MW01484147

THE CROSS MADE *ALL* THE DIFFERENCE

THE CROSS MADE *ALL* THE DIFFERENCE

GERALD MCCRAY

The Cross Made ALL The Difference

A Sunday School Teacher Takes A Closer Look

Series

GERALD MCCRAY

Baby Faith Publishing

ISBN-10: 1985103486
ISBN-13: 978-1985103481

CONTENTS

The Spirit Core Paradigm Shift
Following Faith in *The* Cross

From	**To**
Deformed (corrupted)	Transformed (perfect)
Eternal Death	Eternal Life
Enemy of God	Child of the Living God
Far From God	**Made** Near To Him (He doesn't un-make)
Condemned	Justified
Wicked (twisted thinking)	Righteous (the mind of Christ)
Wickedness (positioned in satan)	Righteousness (Christ positioned within)
Guilty	Innocent
At War With God	Have Peace In God
Dead In Sin	Alive In The Spirit
Sinner	Saint
Sinner "Saved? By Grace"	Joint Heir With Christ
Imprisoned in darkness	Free In God's Kingdom
Victim of Darkness	Victorious In Jesus

The *Spirit Core Paradigm Shift (SCPS) Following Faith In **The** Cross* on the page to the left is a graphic I developed while working on the mother manuscript to *this* book. *Whatever Happened To The Cross?* is a challenging book. It challenges the way the church has traditionally ignored exactly what the Word of the Living God says about the spiritual identity of the *new creation believer.* (2nd Corinthians 5:17/Galatians 6:15) For example, on the third line from the bottom of the SCPS you see a reference to a teaching and longstanding sentiment known as **sinner saved by grace**. There is only one problem with that designation. It is not Bible.

Once Almighty God *justifies the ungodly* (Romans 4:5) at the moment they put faith in *The* Cross, blood, and name of Yeshua Jesus; the Word only refers to that formerly ungodly person in a number of similar ways BUT never sinner. Saint, child of the Almighty God, royal priest, in Christ, and no longer **sin slaves** (Romans 6:6) are a few of the spiritual identity scriptures which converts to Yeshua Jesus are to base their confidence in. In the Bible, the word confidence is almost exclusively translated "faith." Putting faith in fact that Jesus' Cross and blood was payment enough to eliminate your sin debt to Almighty God **instantaneously** shifts your spirit core paradigm from a dead spirit to a spirit core which has been resurrected by and with the Spirit of Christ. (Ephesians 2:1/Colossians 2:13)

Yes, Almighty God wants us to put faith in what His Word says about us. All of us. The ungodly and the saint. From the cradle to the grave. From dead in violations and sin to alive in Messiah Jesus. From enemy of Almighty God (Romans 8:7/Ephesians 2:15-16/James 4:4) (because of the inherited sin nature) to partaker of Almighty God's divine nature (2nd Peter 1:4) through *The* Cross, the blood, the name, and the resurrection of Yeshua Jesus.

That's right, the Word of the Living God is given to the world so that we all would be confident in the **fact** that God loves us all as much as He loves Jesus according to John 17:22-23. "You should take a bite sized chunk of this book and put into an smaller quicker read for the new convert," is what someone said to me while discussing the benefits of *Whatever Happened To The Cross?* I had considered it months before and decided that justification and sanctification were the most important elements of the book which needed to be made bite sized. They are also the most ignored and mistaken facets of the faith. Wrong teaching equals fake faith, (1st

Timothy 1:5/2nd Timothy 1:5) fake believers, (2nd Corinthians 11:26) and fake religion masquerading as science.(1st Timothy 6:20)

In regard to the SCPS graphic, sin will keep you in the column on the left. The lies of the devil will keep you in the column on the left. Sadly, religion has teamed up with condemnation and false humility to keep you in the column on the left. Condemnation will make you "FEEL" like you didn't get justified. It will make you "FEEL" like you are not sanctified. False humility will make you "FEEL" like you were not made the righteousness of Almighty God IN Messiah Jesus. (2nd Corinthians 5:21) The Word of the Living God who cannot lie (Numbers 23:19/Titus 1:2/Hebrews 6:18) says to all of us to spark and challenge and establish our faith confidence in His Word with this scripture:

...let God be true but every man a liar...
Romans 3:4b

Regardless of what you "FEEL" or even know about yourself through your emotions, senses, and natural means, even you must confess that Almighty God's Word is true and what I think I know about myself is a lie. The Almighty God who cannot lie calls you His child, a royal priest, holy person, divine partaker of His nature, and a saint because you have been saved by His grace. To build your faith and confidence in your new creation identity you must repeat what His Word says about you. You can find the few scriptures which I referred to over the last couple pages you read and start there. You can read the seventeenth chapter of John's gospel slowly and repeat what you hear there.

Religion, condemnation, and false humility have led to countless (the Almighty only knows) converts wasting precious time on the hamster wheel hopelessly trying to work for something no one can earn. Jesus' Cross, blood, name, and resurrection have settled the bill. The sin debt is paid. The only contribution we can make to our salvation is simply accepting what Jesus has already accomplished for us. Praying the prayers of Romans 10:9-10 work. "Yes Jesus, Yes," would suffice as well. Jesus did all the work while we were still sin slaves dead in violations and could do nothing to contribute. Religion goads us into working for something that was already given to us. What a shame!

An example or type and shadow of how simple salvation in *The* Cross would be is seen in Numbers 21 and referenced by Yeshua Jesus in

His famous talk with Nicodemus in the third chapter of John's gospel.

*So Moses made a bronze snake and put it on a pole. Anyone who had been bitten would **look** at the bronze snake **and be healed**.*

Numbers 21:9 TEV

And as Moses in the wilderness lifted up the bronze image of a serpent on a pole, even so I must be lifted up upon a pole, so that anyone who believes in me will have eternal life.

John 3:14-15 TLB

Simply looking at a bronze serpent on a pole resulted in the immediate healing of the snake bite victims. Jesus' Cross, blood, name, and resurrection give us something at which to *look and live* and faith in what Jesus did is a effortless as looking, receiving, and being made righteous.

CHAPTER ONE

WHAT NOW?

*Beloved, **now we are children of God**; and it has not yet been revealed what we shall be, but we know that when He is revealed, we shall be like Him, for we shall see Him as He is. And everyone who has this hope in Him purifies himself, just as He is pure.*

1 John 3:2-3

Now that you have given God your heart and the preacher your hand; what now? Okay, you got saved but why? For what? The Word of God tells us in Proverbs 8:36, Romans 5:12, and Ephesians 2:1 [to name a few] that we all are dead in sins and enemies of Almighty God because of Adam's sin. The fifth chapter of

Romans teaches that Adam's sin passed on to all humanity making us all guilty before Almighty God. (Romans 3:19)   God sacrificed His Son Jesus on the altar of *The* Cross as payment for the sin debt of all humanity.   Putting faith in *The* Cross, the blood, and the name of Jesus results in us being credited with the exoneration which Jesus received after being raised from the dead. I know that sounds like a lot but as you progress in your Christian walk, you will learn more and more about God, the Word, Jesus, the Holy Spirit, prayer, and many more aspects of this new peaceful relationship you have with the Almighty God.   Peace with God because He laid the punishment for all of our iniquities and sins upon Jesus on *The* Cross.

*All we like sheep have gone astray; We have turned, every one, to his own way; And **the Lord has laid on Him the iniquity of us all***.

Isaiah 53:6

This book is an excerpt of a larger work called *Whatever Happened To The Cross?* The reason for this work is to be a bit of a quick start guide for new believers; giving them small bites of spiritual nutrition and knowledge. When you can, read the entire 53rd chapter of Isaiah's prophecy to get a complete picture of Jesus' suffering on your behalf. The reason that it is important to get a complete picture is to underpin the critical understanding of the extent to which Heaven went to rescue us from the Almighty God's judgment on sin and the sin nature.

The **Spirit Core Paradigm Shift Following Faith In The Cross** graphic following the Contents page is a sort of cheat sheet for your benefit. It conveys just a few of the most important aspects of the benefits of putting faith in the rescue plan the Almighty God has accomplished through His Son Yeshua/Jesus. The main benefit of this graphic is that it saves you from wasting valuable time on **the hamster wheel of condemnation**. Condemnation is that debilitating feeling you will experience IF you engage in the former sinful behaviors which you have been saved from. Sinful behaviors which Jesus was already punished for.

Condemnation makes you feel hopeless about being a real Christian when you sin because you rightly expect to be a better person and to do better after your come to Jesus moment.

There is therefore now no condemnation to those

who are in Christ Jesus, who do not walk according to the flesh, but according to the Spirit.

Romans 8:2

The Word of the Living God tells us that we are His children the moment we put faith in *The* Cross. The moment we accept the love which the Living Father has for us (1st John 4:16) and accept the Lordship of Yeshua Jesus (Romans 10:9-10); we are **right now** the children of the Living God who created the Heavens and the Earth. We are now the children of the God of the Bible. The Living God of Abraham is now our God and now our Father. The patriarch Abraham was known as "the Friend of God," (James 2:23). What an impressive statement.

Over the years, I have seen many people marvel at that statement. They envy the idea of such a relationship as friend of God but don't get excited about themselves being a *Child of God*. Fathers value and cherish their children far and away more than they do their friends. Once he heard Jesus' sermon in the Paradise suburb of Hell (Psalm 22:22); do you think Abraham was more excited to now be the Living God's child because of *The* Cross or wanted to keep the lesser relationship of friend?

*12 But to as many as did receive him, to those who put their trust in his person and power, he gave the **right to become children of** [the Living] God,*
13 not because of bloodline, physical impulse or human intention, but because of God.

John 1:12-13 CJB

Matthew 6:14   *"...your Heavenly Father..."*
Matthew 6:26   *"...your Heavenly Father..."*
Matthew 6:32   *"...your Heavenly Father..."*
Luke 11:13   *"...your Heavenly Father..."*

As exciting as those assurances are; John 20:21 takes the family connection far above to an exceedingly abundant excitement. Jesus appears to His disciples on Resurrection Day after Mary of Magdala told them that He had risen. Jesus appears out of thin air, it seemed, and this follows:

*Then said Jesus to them again, Peace be unto you: as **my** Father hath sent me, even so send I you.*

If you read this verse in a King James Bible, you will find that the word "my" is italicized. In the opening reference pages of the earliest printings of the original KJV Bible, the

GERALD McCRAY

translators' notes explained that when you find words in italics; understand that they were added because either part of the manuscript was missing or the translators felt a thought was truncated.   Before *The* Cross, Jesus called the Living God, "my Father,"   "your Father", and taught us to begin prayer with, " our Father." After *The* Cross, Jesus addresses His disciples saying, "As Father has sent Me..." Who talks to other people like that? Only family members. Even close cousins speaking to each other about their Dads say, "my dad or your dad," but when siblings are speaking to each other they simply say, "Dad said..."

Do you see it?   Look and live!

After   *The*   Cross...after   Hell...after   the resurrection,   Jesus   refers   to   us...talks   to us...addresses us as His siblings. *"Just as Father sent Me so I am sending you."* WOW!

The Cross made us blood relatives with Yeshua/Jesus. The Messiah of the world is sibling to those redeemed by faith in the grace of *The* Cross.

The *Champion of Israel* (Revelation 20:9) is elder

17

brother to those of us who have received the charis (grace) of *The* Cross. The same *blood which shall never lose its power* is running through our spiritual veins. The resurrected human spirit is in dialysis with *The* Cross of Christ. We simply need to put faith in Jesus' work before, on, and after the cross. Yes, after the cross. Jesus went to Hell (Psalms 22:12-25, Matthew 12:40, Acts 2:27, Ephesians 4:8-9) so that you and I would not have to. Jesus took our place on our cross and even took our place in Hell and suffered the equivalent of eternal judgment so that we would not have to. So, the use of the term *The* Cross means so much more than Jesus' death on that tree. So much more than the device on which His body died.

The Cross made us heirs of the Living God of creation and joint heirs with our sibling Messiah. Have we learned anything like that from religion? Have we learned anything like that from traditional church services? To be fair; we have alluded to it like some superficial cliché but failed to delve deep into its real meaning. Have we learned anything like that from filling up on news commentary programs? We definitely haven't learned anything like that from false humility. False humility tells us that the affirming portions of scripture couldn't possibly mean what they say. Especially to wretched worms saved by grace.

The Word of the Living God promises us the indwelling of the Holy Spirit with an accompanying prayer language called *praying in the Spirit.* (Jude 20) It is also referred to as *praying in [unlearned] tongues* or *speaking in [unlearned] tongues.* (Acts 2:8/1st Corinthians 14) Religion says that tongues passed away with the Apostles along with miracles. Religion says that tongues is of the devil. False humility, on the other hand, convinces others that tongues are for special Christians while the Word says that it is for all of God's children. **Right now!** The Word says that tongues will cease once Jesus returns. Until then, every believer should exercise the Heavenly prayer language.

For he who speaks in a tongue does not speak to men but to God, for no one understands him; however, in the spirit he speaks mysteries.

1 Corinthians 14:2

We have trouble accepting what the Word tells us about ourselves even while reading it right from the Bible with our own eyes. The only way religion and false humility work so well against the church is IF the people don't read and study the scriptures for themselves. The few who do read for themselves are sometimes duped into not thinking for themselves. The Word is clear that the Holy Spirit will teach THE TRUTH from the inside out and help us to understand it.(John 16:13) To understand the pictures of amazing grace, righteousness, justification, and the **right now** realities.

The images which the Word of God paint of our new creation spirit core seem so fantastic and lofty and we hold those up to the images we have of ourselves. The result is sometimes as simple as ignoring those things or expecting them to happen later on…in the sweet by and by. The eighteenth verse of the third chapter of 2nd Corinthians says that we don't have to wait for the sweet by and by to understand our new identity.

17 Now the Lord is that Spirit: and where the Spirit of the Lord is, there is liberty.
*18 But **we all**, with open face beholding as in a glass the glory of the Lord, **are changed into the same image** from glory to glory, even as by the Spirit of the Lord.*   2 Corinthians 3:17-18

The indwelling Spirit of the Living God is using the Word and revelation of who and what we are in our new creation spirit core to transform us into the same image of that glory picture we see in the Word. But here is what blows my religious mind away:

*We...beholding **as in a [mirror]**...are changed into the same image of glory.*

The first chapter of James' letter to the church at large contrasts the difference between the person who is trapped in religion and the person who is fighting the good fight of faith for relationship with the Almighty God. Religion has you thinking that grace is too good to be true and that you MUST contribute to your salvation. Relationship is found in the mirror of the *Perfect Law of Liberty*.

22 And remember, it is a message to obey, not just to listen to. So don't fool yourselves.
23 For if a person just listens and doesn't obey, he is like a man looking at his face in a mirror;
24 as soon as he walks away, he can't see himself anymore or remember what he looks like.
*25 But if anyone **keeps looking steadily** into God's law for free men, he will not only remember it but he will do what it says, and God will greatly bless him in everything he does.*

26 Anyone who says he is a Christian but doesn't control his sharp tongue is just fooling himself, and his religion isn't worth much.

James 1:22-26 TLB

People who have been trapped in religious thinking for too long find teachings of the Almighty's grace and goodness as heresy and blasphemous. When Jesus preached His first sermon in His home town following His wilderness temptation; He simply read the scripture from Isaiah about how good God wants to be to everyone and the religious leaders escorted Jesus to a cliff to throw Him off head first. The scripture actually says that Jesus "*began to speak gracious words*" and they wanted to get rid of Him. He barely got started before they interrupted His sermon.

The Almighty's mirror tells you that your spirit core is perfect now through faith in The Cross but the religious and carnal minds say that is too good to be true. I have the same proclivities, eccentricities, and cravings which I had before. How can my spirit be perfect? The Almighty's mirror tells you what you spirit is like after it has been washed in the blood of the Lamb. What you are struggling with is the rest of you. Your soul, mind, emotions, and body.

*Now may the God of peace Himself sanctify you completely; and may **your whole spirit, soul**, and **body** be preserved blameless at the coming of our Lord Jesus Christ. He who calls you is faithful, who also will do it.*   1 Thessalonians 5:23-24

Meditate on these things; give yourself entirely to them, that your progress may be evident to all. Take heed to yourself and to the doctrine. Continue in them, for in doing this you will save both yourself and those who hear you.

1 Timothy 4:15-16

Finding your identity in the Word of Almighty God is the first step to breaking free and staying free from religion. Saying about yourself what He says about you is critical. Your religious mind will rebel and part of you will call you a liar and hypocrite for "saying things you know are not true!" But remember that the Almighty cannot and will not lie; so say what He says about you based on what His Word says without adding subtle changes to it. Eventually, your confidence will get to the point where you are totally persuaded that you are who and what He says you are and not what religion, condemnation, false humility and cable news says about you.

The Living God's glory which reflected off of Moses' face was the wake of glory which he saw as God walked pass him.(Exodus 33:18-23) We, *THE REDEEMED*, not only have the right to view the glory face to face in the Word; we also have the glory deposited inside our spirit core. Maybe I am taking reasoning (Isaiah 1:18) to an extreme but when I consider that statement made in 2nd Corinthians 3:18, I find it interesting that the Word doesn't simply say *in a mirror* but *AS in a mirror*. Why is it worded like this?

In the first letter to the Corinthians, Paul tells them that he wanted to teach them the meat of the Word and the deep things of God but because he knew that they couldn't bear it he would continue giving them the milk. In this second letter to the Corinthians, Paul serves meat but gives them little bite size pieces to work on. When he says that they couldn't bear the meaty things he wanted to share with them; it sounds like one of Jesus' final conversations with His disciples before His commenced the suffering this author terms *The* Cross.

Paul wanted the readers in Corinth to connect the dots. If they submitted to the reasoning process (Isaiah 1:18, John 16:8) of the Holy Spirit; He would have taken their learning and comprehension to the conclusions which the

Lord wanted to share with His disciples in the sixteenth chapter of John's gospel.

*12 "I still have many things to say to you, **but you cannot bear them now**.*
13 However, when He, the Spirit of truth, has come, He will guide you into all truth; for He will not speak on His own authority, but whatever He hears He will speak; and He will tell you things to come.
14 He will glorify Me, for He will take of what is Mine and declare it to you.   John 16:12-14

When the Holy Spirit, the Spirit of truth, comes; "*He will complete the teaching and training which I started*," is the feeling I get from Jesus' statement. In conjunction with the following scriptures, we can conclude that Jesus was referring to Himself taking up residence in every new creation believer. Yes!
*Neither shall they say, Lo here! or, lo there! for, behold, **THE KINGDOM OF GOD IS WITHIN YOU**.*
Luke 17:21

*I **IN THEM AND YOU IN ME**; that they may be made perfect in one, and that the world may know that You have sent Me, **and have loved them as You have loved Me**.*   John 17:23

I made you known to them, and I will continue to do so, in order that the love you have for me may be in them, and **SO THAT I ALSO MAY BE IN THEM***."* John 17:26 TEV

And what agreement hath the temple of God with idols? for ye are the temple of the living God; as God hath said, **I WILL DWELL IN THEM***, and walk* **in them***; and I will be their God, and they shall be my people.* 2 Corinthians 6:16

To whom God would make known what is the riches of the glory of this **[secret]** *among the Gentiles; which is* **CHRIST IN YOU***, the hope of glory.* Colossians 1:27

Look at what the *Word of Truth* (Psalms 119:43/2 Corinthians 6:7/Ephesians 1:13/2 Timothy 2:15/James 1:18) has to say about the new creation believer. ABOUT YOU. About me. About every child of the Living God. Religion convinces us that we have to work enough, pray enough, worship enough, feed enough needy, and behave just right to obtain what Jesus already gave to us. What Jesus already obtained for us through His suffering, His cross, and His blood. Ephesians 1:11 says that we have obtained an inheritance IN CHRIST (verse 10).

False humility attempts to convince us that we are not there yet although the Word of Truth says, "*has obtained*."[past tense]   False humility says that we are not worthy. We are just worms, wretches, and could never think that what Jesus said about us is true. How sadly deceptive is that? **Jesus only tells the truth.**

The devilish duo of religion and false humility either wants us to imagine these great things happening later, eventually, and in the sweet by and by. False humility wants you to "*get worthy*"(perform) to   receive those promises which are already given to Jesus and by imputable default to us. This duo wants to distract us from the most important aspect of our salvation. The most exciting proclamation of *The* Cross – Now.

Now! now! now!   Right now!

Religion and false humility want to nullify *knowledge of the glory* (2ND Corinthians 4:6) which the Most High God has deposited in the resurrected spirit core of the new creation believer.   They want us to focus on our superficial traits and behaviors but *The* Cross didn't start its work on the surface. *The* Cross works deep. "*A new spirit will I put in them*," the

Living Father promised in Ezekiel chapters eleven and thirty six. The Living God had Ezekiel predict the indwelling twice. Not for the sweet by and by but for the nasty here and now. Right now! First John 3:2 says that RIGHT NOW we are the children of the Living God.

When are we the children of the Living God?

Right Now!

The main reason religion and false humility take our focus off of now is because NOW FAITH IS according to Hebrews 11:1. Faith works now. Faith comes by the hearing and hearing by the Word of God NOW. Our Loving Father wants us to imagine NOW is when His Word to us is being manifested.

Right now we have eternal life (John 3:18/6:54)

When do we have eternal life?   _____!

Right now we are engraved on God's hands
                                (Isaiah 49:16/John 10:28)

When are we engraved on God's hands?
_____!

Right now our lives are hid with Christ in God

(Colossians 3:3)

When are our lives hid with Christ in God?

_____!

Right now are we seated with Christ in Heaven

(Ephesians 2:6)

When are we seated with Christ in Heaven?

_____

Right now are we blessed with all spiritual blessings (Ephesians 1:3)

When are we blessed with all spiritual blessings?

_____

Right now are we partakers of God's divine nature (2nd Corinthians 3:18/2nd Peter 1:3-4)

When are we partakers of God's divine nature?

_____

Did you fill in your blanks? **Did you add your own exclamation points to the last three?** Do you understand why religion has to die? The head injury kept me from bringing *The Death of Religion* manuscript over. Can you see that false humility is a deception of pride just as self righteousness is? Self righteousness is about your personal performance to gain grace which cannot be earned.(Romans 11:6) Pride is saying that I am much too bad for God's Grace to lift me up out of my putrid sin nature. What that mentality says is that the Loving Father's grace can't reach those depths of depravity. These are the typical responses from those who think they are too bad for God's amazing grace to save:

"I'm not worthy."   True!
"I'm not good enough."   True!
"You don't know where I've been."   True!
"You don't know just how bad I've been."   And?

YOU AND ME BEING UNWORTHY is not a news flash to Heaven. Almighty God justifies the ungodly! Not the worthy. It is a legal decree from God Himself.

IF YOU WERE WORTHY then there would be no need for *The* Cross. God justifies the ungodly! Not the worthy. We can't justify ourselves.

BECAUSE WE ARE NOT WORTHY that makes *The* Cross absolutely necessary to justify the ungodly. If we could justify ourselves, Jesus wouldn't have suffered what He did. The fact of *The* Cross is proof positive that there was no other way.

The fact that the gift of **the Spirit** or presence **of the Living God** has been not only given to us but resides **inside unworthy us** is a glaring testament to the exceeding abundant surpassing richness of grace which was dumped on us. Data dump in our spirit core? An amount of grace which cannot be merely termed as amazing when it has afforded the ungodly a place in the inner circle of the Godhead and even "broken off" a part of the "God stuff"(2 Peter 1:4) so that we can take it.

If you thought you were worthy of God's grace then that thought would immediately disqualify you from receiving it. Heaven knows we are not worthy and that is why Jesus imparted His worthiness into our resurrected spirit core. He went far and above that and transferred the glory which the Father gave Him into our resurrected spirit core.

You should listen to Brad Scott's [WildBranch Ministries] teaching called *In My Flesh* on the Hebraic Roots Network (HRN) via the App Store, Play Store, YouTube or Roku. His teaching correlates the roles of messenger RNA and transfer RNA with the redemptive and atoning work of Christ. It is absolutely amazing. I think it was eight lectures in total and a few of them I watched multiple times. You biology majors and tech heads will be evangelized by a lecture on DNA. I dare you to watch it and not find the Living God. The Hebrew alephbet is seasoning these lectures quite well...as well. That was the best tangent yet. Back to the subject.

Heaven knows we are not worthy and still says in 2nd Corinthians 3:18 that RIGHT NOW we are being changed into the same glorious image of the glorious Son of the glorious Living God. There is not enough religious activity and "busy work" of charity which we can do to earn that. False humility needs to be evicted from our minds, churches, and teaching so that we can embrace true humility. **True humility believes what the Word of God says and receives it** no matter how uncomfortable it is to our natural and religious mentality.

Find your Heavenly Father's exceeding and precious promises to you, for you, in you, and through you and receive them all RIGHT NOW.

By simply saying, "*Yes, Jesus. Yes!*"

And repent of the old life, vow never to return to

it, and ask and receive His help to do just that.

From that time Jesus began to preach and to say, "Repent, for the kingdom of heaven is at hand."
                                    Matthew 4:17 NKJV

Yes, Jesus. Yes!

Yes!

CHAPTER TWO

JUST IF I'D *NEVER* SINNED?

*Now to him that works [for justification] is the reward not reckoned of grace, but [wages earned]. But to him that [doesn't work to earn it], but believes on [**the Father** which] **justifies the ungodly**, his faith is counted for righteousness.*
Romans 4:4-5

    I did not do well with algebraic equations in the beginning. The second time I took on the algebra challenge; I brought my grade up from *F* to *D*. Although I hadn't failed it again, a *D* still felt like failure. It was progress for me but I knew I could do better. I imagined myself doing better. The third time, I think I got it up to a low *B* or high *C*. Isn't it interesting that remembering failures with stark detail is so easy? Successes not so much.

When I got to geometry, I was ready for equations and did quite well. I have been inspired by the Word of God to think scientifically. As a new Christian studying the scriptures; I remember telling my mother, "The universe is still growing because God never told the light to stop." (Genesis 1:3) "That's nice, take out the trash," she said. Romans 4:4-5 has inspired an equation.

$$U + F/C = EL$$

or

Ungodly + Faith in *The* Cross = Zöë

Zöë is the Greek word for eternal life (EL). John 10:10 is where the word Zöë was used by Jesus to refer to eternal life. The life of the Living God. The power of an endless life (Hebrews 7:16) is deposited into the heart of the ungodly the moment they put faith in *The* Cross. Why is this understanding so important? Being right with the Living God is all His work and none of ours. Once we accept His love and the Lordship of Yeshua/Jesus; the Living God becomes our Living Father. Religion hates faith in *The* Cross because faith gives religion nothing to do. Nothing to contribute.

The religion trap burdens church people with a carrot and stick system which doesn't work. Religion offers a feeling of assurance resulting from performing for the church, other people, and even Heaven. Reading ten pages from the Bible must be twice as good as reading five. Attending church three times per week must be three times better than going only once per week. The more religious, devotional, and spiritual activities I engage in must make me a better Christian...right? Wrong!

*28 Come to Me, all you who **labor** and are **heavy laden**, and I will give you rest.*
29 Take My yoke upon you and learn from Me, for I am gentle and lowly in heart, and you will find rest for your souls.
30 For My yoke is easy and My burden is light."
Matt 11:28-30 NKJV

Of course, Jesus was talking about more than religion; but keep in mind that He was speaking to the most religious people in the world when He gave this invitation. The Law is a system of religious performance. People under the Law were right with God based on their performance. Based on what they did. Under this grace covenant which Jesus sealed in His blood; people are right with the Living God based on Jesus' performance. We are right with the Living God based on what Jesus did. That is why His burden is light; because He has already done all the heavy lifting. His yoke is easy because He is pulling with you. The theme scripture of this chapter says that justification cannot be earned. The only way to get justified by the Living God is through believing. Believing what? Believing that the Living God justifies the ungodly.

That doesn't even make sense. Wouldn't it make sense to think that devout and busy church people are more likely to get justified rather than the ungodly? We cannot earn justification. If it could be earned; then it would be payment for services rendered. Because it cannot be earned then it all depends on the Living God, Jesus' works, mercy, and grace. *Grace, grace, God's grace. Grace that is greater than all our sin*! Amen!

The reason religion is so prevalent and dangerous is because we are comfortable working for righteousness. The only problem is only one person was able to keep the Law perfectly – Jesus. Depending on the mercy and grace of the Living God is less taxing than working for righteousness. The Living God doesn't justify workers, laborers, and those overburdened with ceremony and spiritual anxiety. **He justifies the ungodly**. That is so important to understand. If you get right with the Living God; it is not because you earned it but because you simply received what Jesus earned for you. Wow! Wow! Wow!

The most interesting Old Testament story line which *bleeds* into the New Testament began in the Sumerian culture. Abraham, when he was still known as Abram, received an invitation from the Living God to leave his home and join Him on an adventure which would prove to change the course of human history in so many ways. Abraham's most notable descendant, Yeshua Jesus, would prove so impactful on human nature and human history that recorded time would pivot on His life. Yeshua Jesus lived on earth for approximately 30 years before beginning His public redemption ministry. His three-year ministry has impacted the world in such magnitude; that it still transforms lives to this day.

The most effective charities, benevolent outreaches, and even medical strategies incorporate elements of His ministry nearly two thousand years after His death. A death which lasted for such a brief period that He borrowed a tomb and vacated it after the "weekend" was over.

The reports of His resurrection have been instrumental in founding churches, religious organizations, and institutional denominations the world over. Lives have been undeniably changed following the "hear ye hear ye" proclamations regarding the risen Savior. Those listeners in parts of the world which haven't been inundated with religious tradition, as Americans have, witness the miraculous flow of that resurrection power which *The* Cross placed in every new creation believer. I recall hearing a sermon which included this statement:

"If Baptists know anything, it is how to get people saved," because traditionally all we preach is salvation. We preach salvation and people get saved. What if we preached the rest of the gospel? What if we preached healing and miracles?"

It is amazing how such a solitary life as Jesus of Nazareth's is impacting humanity. His resurrection, it turns out, was the capstone of His redemption ministry. Not only did He predict the details of His death but He also predicted His resurrection.

He assured His listeners that He would die at His own behest and raise Himself from the dead in the same manner. A beneficial outcome of the resurrection, is something called justification which is a legal term. To be justified or declared righteous by the *Righteous Judge* (2nd Timothy 4:8) of the universe means to be treated **as if you never sinned and never had the sin nature**. When the One who said, "Light be," calls you justified; it carries the legal benefits of being found innocent.

7 I have fought a good fight, I have finished my course, I have kept the faith:
*8 Hereafter there is laid up for me **a crown** of righteousness, **which the Lord**, the righteous judge, **shall give** me at that day: and not to me only, but un**to all them also that love his appearing**.* 2 Timothy 4:7-8

Part of the *good fight of faith* is resisting the discordant voices of religious tradition, (Matthew 15:6/Mark 7:13) false humility, worldly influence, (Romans 12:2) and doctrines of devils. (1ˢᵗ Timothy 4:1)   According to Romans 8:1-2, condemnation has no legitimate place in the life of the new creation believer. Condemnation abides in religion and false humility. Condemnation is used to ignite performance of the individual; all the while ignoring faith in Jesus' performance.

Before *The* Cross, broken humanity was slave to the dark spirit in a domain or kingdom of darkness. Jesus said in John 8:44 that the devil is the father of the spiritually dead. Jesus said that the devil is also the father of lies, liars, haters, and murderers.   After *The* Cross, the *accuser of the believers* (Revelation 12:10) uses condemnation to feign the old slavery and bondage of sin. Although it is not real bondage; it has the potential to entangle the new believer in works and acts of contrition to "feel" assured that one is right with God again. The problem with that thinking is that it ignores how the ungodly got justified in the first place. Faith, not works. Not feelings.

What got the ungodly right with the Living God is the same thing which will give the "sinning saint" assurance that they are right with their new Spirit Father once they repent of the sin out loud to God and put faith in His Word which says, "*If we confess our sins, he is faithful and just and will forgive us our sins and purify us from all unrighteousness.* (1st John 1:9 NIV) And once all unrighteousness is purified, what is left behind?   You guessed it; **only righteousness**. Faith at salvation cleanses the sin stained soul and faith in *The* Cross after salvation cleanses the conscience of condemnation and uncertainty of righteousness. The following scriptures are a great starting place for understanding the exciting provision of Jesus' blood being able to purge our conscience of condemnation and of a wretch mentality as well as the traditional *I'm not worthy* banner of false humility.

Which was a figure for the time then present, in which were offered both gifts and sacrifices, that **could not make** *him that did the service* **perfect**, *as* **pertaining to the conscience**;   Hebrews 9:9

13 For if the blood of bulls and of goats, and the ashes of an heifer sprinkling the unclean, sanctifies to the purifying of the flesh:
14 How much more shall **the blood of Christ**, *who through the eternal Spirit offered himself without spot* **to** *God,* **purge your conscience** *from dead works to serve the living God*?   Hebrews 9:13-14

For the law *having a shadow of good things to*

come, and not the very image of the things, **can never with those sacrifices** *which they offered year by year continually make the comers thereunto perfect.*

2 For then would they not have ceased to be offered? because that the worshippers once **purge***d should have had no more* **conscience of sins***.* Hebrews 10:1-2

21 And having an high priest over the house of God;

22 Let us draw near with a true heart **in full assurance of faith***, having our hearts sprinkled from an evil conscience, and our bodies washed with pure water.* Hebrews 10:21-22

Because of Jesus' cross, each individual can be severed from that spiritually dead relationship and be adopted by the Righteous Judge (2nd Timothy 4:8) according to Romans 8, Galatians 4, and Ephesians chapter one. We also **are severed from the slavery of condemnation** and guilty consciences. Completely cleansed of a sin consciousness. Glory! Glory! Glory! *The* Cross frees us from the hamster wheel of condemnation.

Did you get that? You can be adopted by the same One who declares you righteous, justified, innocent, and perfect. All of the cards are stacked in your "FAVOR" - a synonym for grace. Yes, grace! Jesus did us a priceless favor on *The* Cross. Again, we see why it is described as amazing. Let's take a closer look at justification.

Because of our sins [Jesus] was given over to die, and He was raised to life in order to put us right with God.   Romans 4:25 TEV

The fourth chapter of Paul's letter to the Romans summarizes the faith adventure God invited Abraham on. The case is clearly made that Abraham was made right with God through faith and because Abraham simply believed what God had promised him, Abraham had righteousness [right standing with God] attributed to him. A closer look at Abraham's life and we are hard pressed to see the righteousness.

The Word makes it clear in 1st Samuel 16:7 that, "*The Lord sees not as man sees; for man looks on the outward appearance, but the Lord looks on the heart.*" Thank the Living LORD for that because Colossians 1:27 tells us new creation believers that the Son of the Living God is in the heart [spirit core] of the new creation believer. The LORD sees Him and not us. Thank

God! Does that mean that the devil knows the new creation believer better than we know ourselves? Is that why he attempts to get us to believe wrongly? To focus on superficial behaviors and failures to distract us from the real change deep within at our spirit core.

On the surface Abraham looked like all of us. He was a liar when it meant saving his own skin at the risk of his wife being violated in an Egyptian harem. "When they ask who we are." Abraham instructed his wife, "say brother and sister." He went on to explain the common practice of killing husbands and imprisoning the widows in harems. This was his justification for the lie. Who wouldn't do what Abraham did? He was just like the rest of us.

Still, something puzzling is said about lying Abraham in Isaiah 41:8 and reiterated in James 2:23. Abraham is called, "The friend of God."[i] Really?

As questionable as Abraham's actions were, he was still called God's friend. But how?

*3 For the Scriptures tell us, "Abraham **believed God**, and God counted him as righteous **because of his faith**."*
4 When people work, their wages are not a gift, but something they have earned.

5 But people are counted as righteous, not because of their work, but because of their faith in God who forgives sinners. Romans 4:3-5

In verse four above we understand that religious works (intended to "get" from God) and grace (taking what Jesus got for us) don't mix.

Romans 4:16 says that, "*...justification is of faith that it might be by grace.*" **It wasn't what Abraham did which made him right with God but what Abraham believed**. Abraham's faith/confidence in God's promises resulted in grace and, as The Hoppers sing, "*Grace Will Always Be Greater Than Sin.*" If we continue to put faith in *The* Cross; the blood of Jesus will **continue to cleanse us** according to 1st John 1:7.

If you read earlier verses of that chapter, you will conclude that being free of sin consciousness and being continually washed by *The* Cross allows us to fellowship with the Father and the Son, no doubt, with the admission of the sanctifying Holy Spirit within.

Does that mean that it was really what God did that made Abraham righteous? Don't make the mistake of concluding that actions don't matter because Abraham's faith which is referenced here is faith which he put into action.

When the angel stopped Abraham from sacrificing his "only" son Isaac; the angel said, "I know now that you [reverence and honor God]. In other words, "I see your faith Abraham." Although it is what Abraham believed which made him right with the Living God; the corresponding action exhibited on the outside reflected the faith which was on the inside. Think about that. Anyone familiar with Abraham's story might ask about the other son. Isaac is called Abraham's only son by the Living God three times in the twenty second chapter of Genesis. Didn't He know that there was another son?

Abraham was promised by the Living God to sire a son with his wife Sarah. Because Sarah was about ninety years old when Abraham received the promise; she laughed. Who wouldn't? A year later Isaac (means laughter) was born. I guess faith got the last laugh.

The son born as a result of human schemes was the natural son. The son birthed by a woman over ninety years of age was called the son of promise. The son God gave Abraham was Isaac. The son the Egyptian servant girl gave Abraham was called the son of the flesh. And His mother's hate for Abraham was passed down through souls and bloodlines.

For if the inheritance be of the law, it is no more of promise: but God gave it to Abraham by promise.
                                            Galatians 3:18

28 Now we...as Isaac was, are the children of promise.
29 But as then he that was born after the flesh persecuted him that was born after the Spirit, even so it is now.   Galatians 4:28-29

In the fifteenth chapter of Genesis, Abraham cut covenant with the Living God. The customary blood oath included both parties either standing in the blood of a large animal or painted with the blood of a small animal. The two parties would pledge all they had including their lives to the other. Something amazing happened in the blood oath Abraham was part of. The amazing thing is that the Living God did all of the talking. While Abraham slept, the Living God, in the form of fire, passed through the blood of the sacrificed animal while making promises to Abraham.

The only way either party could be absolved of the responsibilities and vows of the blood oath was through death. Breaking the blood oath gave the other party the legal right to execute the violator. The God of creation and LORD of light who cannot lie because His nature won't allow it; bound Himself to a blood oath to ignite the faith and confidence of Abraham via primitive man's most trusted transaction. Abraham's faith (which resulted in righteousness) was connected directly to the blood of a blood oath. All that the Living God had was pledged to Abraham; up to and including His own life. Abraham couldn't help but believe it. That blood oath would never be broken because the Eternal God – the self existing One - lives forever.

Abraham's faith was anchored to the blood oath which the Living God made with him. God vow on His life that He would do for Abraham everything He promised. So, when the scripture says, "Abraham believed God and it was credited to him for righteousness," we are being told that Abraham's faith was anchored to the most secure transaction known to man – a blood oath. Abraham was still called Abram until after the blood oath of Genesis fifteen. While Abram slept, the Living God was pledging all He had to Abram including His life.

The Living God told a ninety-nine year old man that he would father a child with his ninety-year-old wife...and it happened. About twenty-eight years later, Abraham was challenged to sacrifice his "only" son, Isaac who posed a good question to his father Abraham. "I see the wood and the altar but where is the sacrifice?"

Abraham answered, "The LORD will provide Himself a lamb for the sacrifice." If you've been in church at least two years; you've' probably heard twenty sermons on that portion of scripture alone. That's right Isaac wasn't a small helpless child. Isaac was referred to as a lad because his daddy was one hundred years older than he. Think about it.

Abraham's statement, "the LORD will provide Himself a sacrifice for offering," was based on his understanding of the blood oath. His answer was based on his ninety-one year old wife giving birth just as God promised. The Living God pledged all He had to Abram and then changed his name to remind him of the promise. From Abram – honored father – to Abraham – father of an innumerable multitude. Abraham's faith was linked to and ***anchored by the blood*** of the covenant. Our faith should be anchored to the blood of *The* Cross.

When the Word of the Living God challenges us to believe the promises of the Living God in the Bible; we are being reminded that the blood sacrifice – *The* Cross – is the anchor of our faith. When we are challenged to let the Word be true and every other voice a lie (Romans 3:4); we anchor our faith to *The* Cross.

No matter how screwed up you feel; if the Word says that the Living God MADE YOU righteousness in Christ Jesus (2nd Corinthians 5:21) then you anchor your "*believer*" to Jesus' cross and believe the Word more than you believe your five senses. More than you believe those dark mirrors. When the mirrors of regret, shame, and religious guilt identify you as a wretched worm; you anchor your faith to *The* Cross and let the Word be true and those other voices a lie.

*Then Aaron took the gold, melted it down, and molded it into the shape of **a calf**. When the people saw it, they exclaimed, "O Israel, these are **the gods** who brought you out of the land of Egypt!"* Exodus 32:4 NLT

The first letter of the Hebrew alephbet is symbolized by a bull as was the pagan Egyptian deity Horus/Baal (known as Ballat/Allat in Nehemiah 2:10/2:19/13:28). One calf idol is referred to as "*the gods.*" They put Jehovah in the mix with Horus/Baal. Wrong! The God of Abraham, Isaac, and Jacob rescued the Hebrews from slavery in an Egyptian culture in which worshipped deities were represented by a statue or figurine. When these Egyptian Hebrews made and worshipped the golden bull at the foot of Mount Sinai they were not trying to be disrespectful to the God of the rescue but were actually attempting to thank Him. (my opinion) One problem was their object of faith was much too small. The other was it was worship pagan style.

Some scholars say that there are 72 names for the Living God and one name reportedly has 216 characters. Even if we understood all His names and could fluently speak them, our understanding of Him would still amount to a rain drop in the ocean of His vastness. Another problem the Hebrew children or spiritual descendants of Abraham had was the fact that they were attempting to worship the Living God in the same way they had worshipped the dead and inanimate gods of their bondage culture. They used their Egyptian way of worshipping idols and figurines to worship the real God. The One, True, and Living God who created et the Heavens and Earth and all that in them is. The "et" is a Hebrew thing. Look it up and be blessed.

Getting His people out of Egypt was easy. The Living God did that in one day. The plagues weren't for the Egyptians but for His people to understand that He is greater than all of the imagined and supposed gods they worshipped in

Egypt. Thousands of years later, He is still working on getting Egypt [the world system and way of thinking] out of His people. On this side of *The* Cross, the teaching, learning, and implementing of the Word pushes the world system out of us.

The reason Moses broke the first set of tablets before sharing the Ten Commandments with the people was to protect the "nation" as a whole from being guilty of breaking the law and also to keep them from perceiving God incorrectly. The golden calf wasn't a violation of having a god before the Living God but missing the fact that the Living God is not natural but Spirit. Psalm 96:4-5 makes it crystal clear that the Living God is not a mere idol. The Living God with seventy-two names which we know of cannot be portrayed by a statue and He would not accept pagan style worship or be corralled with demon deities.. God wanted to expand their vision so the object of their faith would be accurately and firmly placed. Check out Romans 5:1 from the AMP:

THEREFORE, SINCE we are justified (acquitted, declared righteous, and given a right standing with God) through faith, let us [grasp the fact that we] have [the peace of reconciliation to hold and to enjoy] peace with God through our Lord Jesus Christ (Messiah, the Anointed One).   Romans 5:1

With the introduction of the animal sacrifices, the object of faith was blood of the sacrificed animals. The blood of the innocent was covering the sins of the guilty. Our faith on this side of *The* Cross should be accurately and firmly placed in the blood of Christ. The blood of His cross. The blood of God's Lamb. The cross of Christ making men right with God again is the good news. In the 15th chapter of Genesis, Abraham cut covenant with the Living God. The blood of a bull was shed. The type of ceremony, which was held, was the kind in which both parties walked in the blood making promises to the other. Interestingly, the Living God moved back and forth in the blood of the sacrifice, no doubt, making promises while Abraham remained silent. Maybe Abraham was right with God because of what God did and not what Abraham did. Sound like *The* Cross at all?

3 "As surely as I am the living God," says the Sovereign Lord, "you will not repeat this proverb in Israel any more.
4 The life of every person belongs to me, the life of the parent as well as that of the child. The person

who sins is the one who will die.
                    Ezekiel 18:3-4 TEV

The person who sins will die. However, Jesus committed no sin. So, if His death was in place of the guilty does that mean that His perfection replaces the imperfection of the guilty? Does Him accepting the nature of the serpent in innocence mean that the nature or the serpent in us [the sin nature] has to be eradicated because of His innocence? Because He became sin who knew nothing about sin in place of those who are intimately acquainted with sin; are we switching places with Him?

May *God himself,* ***the God of peace,*** ***sanctify*** *you through and through. May* ***your*** *whole* ***spirit, soul*** *and* ***body*** *be kept blameless at the coming of our Lord Jesus Christ.*   1st Thessalonians 5:23 NIV

The Spirit of the Living God transforms our spirit core when it takes up residence in us. The soul still needs to be saved (Hebrews 10:39) or sanctified by the Holy Spirit. The spirit is one thing and the soul is something else. In our spirit core we have been made right with the Living God through faith in Jesus' cross. Just as Abraham had righteousness credited to his spiritual account through faith does it follow that those who are sanctified (Hebrews 10:14), have perfection imputed/credited to their spiritual accounts - to their spirit cores – through faith in *The* Cross? Jesus' perfection is credited to the souls of those who put faith in the price He paid for the remission of their sins.

We know that whoever is born of God does not sin [**produce sin from the perfect spirit core**]*; but he who has been born of God keeps himself, and the wicked one does not touch him.* 1st John 5:18

IF THE HOLY SPIRIT only dwells inside a perfect person; then under this new and better covenant built on better promises (Hebrews 8:6), we have to conclude that Jesus' perfection has been imputed to us. He shared His perfection with us so that He could also share the glory (2nd Corinthians 3:17-18) and the divine nature (2nd Peter 1:4) also.

Under the Old Covenant, the blood of the sacrificed animals covered the sins of the people. Maybe Jesus' perfection covers our imperfection under the New Covenant. The very fact of justification puts us in a legally secure position of being declared not guilty. That lends to the assertion that for us to be declared justified, we must have Jesus' justifying work credited to our spirit core. **Wow!**

That being said, then justification also brings with it the legal benefits of being justified. If I am not guilty and thus received the imparted or imputed righteousness of the Innocent; then I am also entitled to the benefits of being imputably innocent. The Guilty were to be punished, beaten, and humiliated. But since the Innocent has taken the place of the Guilty and has suffered unjustifiably then the Guilty whose place the Innocent has taken receives the opposite of what is deserved. So the Guilty must by legal default receive the reversal of misfortune visited upon the Innocent. The Innocent was beaten thirty nine times and the Word proclaims that each lash translates into a restorative benefit for the Guilty....declared not guilty...innocent even.

It seems like I keep saying the same thing repeatedly but with good reason. After a year or so of teaching Sunday School lessons on righteousness and justification in one form or another; I repeated something one day that I mentioned multiple times and one person said, "I didn't know that" to which I said, "We've been talking about it for over a year." So I asked the class, "Do you see how embedded religion, religious tradition, and religious thinking is in us?"

I went on to admit that although I had been teaching it for many more years than I had been at this particular church that I still struggle with what seems like a dichotomy between what the Word of the Living God says about me and what I "think" I know about myself. I have to remind myself not to fall for true lies. What's true about me from the soul and body perspective don't line up with the truth of the incorruptible seed of the Word which has been planted in my new spirit. Your new spirit.

3 What if some did not have faith? Will their lack of faith nullify God's faithfulness?
4 Not at all! Let God be true, and every man a liar....   Romans 3:3-4a NIV

If the spirit core of the new creation believer produces righteousness and the faith for it; then the fear and doubt must originate in the mind and emotions. I have to say to myself sometimes, "Let God be true and every man a liar," when I am convincing my mind to agree with the Word of God regarding me no matter how contrary the evidence is that I have of myself. Sounds like faith doesn't it? We can believe what we know about ourselves – our old selves – the residue of the old nature – OR we can agree with the image we see in the mirror of God's Word. The substance of things hoped for and the evidence of things not seen? The soul and body can be locked in behaviors of the past during which we had no regret or sin consciousness for doing wrong.

21 If so be that you have heard him, and have been taught by him, as the truth is in Jesus:
*22 That **you put off** concerning the former conversation **the old man**, which is corrupt according to the deceitful lusts;*
23 And be renewed in the spirit of your mind;
*24 And that **you put on the new man**, which after God is created in righteousness and true holiness.*
Ephesians 4:21-24

We are told to "put on" and "put off" instead of praying for our Father to do it. That must mean that it is up to us to do our part to catch up with what He has already done for and in us. How do we "take off" the old nature and "put on" the new one? It has to be with faith right? And it must be connected to the renewing of our minds. No doubt, the practice of deliberately thinking and speaking the Word of the Living God has to be key in helping us keep a governor on the habits of the old nature.

The crossover secular church hymn *Amazing Grace* speaks of being a former wretch, which has been saved by God's amazing grace secured by Jesus' cross. Once grace gets a hold of you it is impossible to be the wretched worm you once were. So, when you make the mistake of thinking you are still the worm you used to be simply "remind" yourself [renew your mind] and that old worm mentality that you are something different now. A new creation in Christ.

*6 Knowing this, that **our old man [the sin nature]** is crucified with him, that the body of sin might be destroyed, that hereafter we should not serve sin.*

7 For he that is dead is freed from sin.

8 Now if we be dead with Christ, we believe that we shall also live with him:

9 Knowing that Christ being raised from the dead dies no more; death has no more control over him.

10 For in that he died, he died unto sin once: but in that he lives, he lives unto God. [FOREVER]

*11 Likewise **reckon you also yourselves to be dead indeed unto sin [the sin nature]**, but alive unto God through Jesus Christ our Lord.* [FOREVER]

*12 **Let not** sin therefore reign in your mortal body, that you should obey it in the lusts thereof.*

Romans 6:6-12

Simply because our unregenerate minds and bodies are conditioned like Pavlov's dogs responding to triggered responses doesn't mean that we are still what we used to be; but simply that our old nature – the old man – rears its sinful head. For the Word of the Living God to say, "Don't let," (Romans 6:12) means we have the ability of resist now. We didn't have that before.

We have a choice now compared to the former bondage of the sin nature. When the old nature rears its desperate head, it is up to us to put it away again. (Ephesians 4:31)   The sin nature, the old man, the former conversation [way of living and talking] is no longer our slave master. *The* Cross of Christ has freed us indeed. That sparks another question though.

20 And when he was demanded of the Pharisees, when the kingdom of God should come, he answered them and said, The kingdom of God does not come with observation:
21 Neither shall they say, Lo here! or, lo there! for,

behold, **the kingdom of God is within you.**

Luke 17:20-21

The Pharisees were the most criticized religious leaders Jesus encountered. Jesus called them out on many occasions for their empty religious practice and desire to be revered by others for their apparent piety and religious devotion. Why would Jesus tell this group that the kingdom of the Living God was within them?

Although they didn't always use the Word of God properly they definitely had it all in them as far as the information or letters go; but they fell short on understanding the spirit of the letters (2 Corinthians 3:6) as was pointed out to them by Messiah Jesus.

The Word mentions many different designations for the sin nature. Wickedness, unrighteous, unholy, unthankful, the old man, children of judgment, and darkness are a few. There must be more than one designation for the new nature. The fact that the Spirit of the Living God would take up residence inside our resurrected and reconnected spirit core must give it a new nature of its own.

15 If you love me, keep my commandments.

16 And I will pray the Father, and he shall give you another Comforter, that he may abide with you forever;

*17 Even the Spirit of truth; whom the world cannot receive, because it sees him not, neither knows him: but you know him; for he dwells with you, and **shall be in you**.*

*18 I will not leave you comfortless: **I will come to you**.*   John 14:15-18

Jesus promised His disciples the indwelling of the kingdom Spirit of the Living God. He told them that the Holy Spirit would reside inside them. This was so different from the Old Testament operation of the Holy Spirit who spent most of the Old Testament behind a thick curtain in the mobile tabernacles and later the "permanent" temples. It wasn't God's original intention for the Spirit to remain penned up but He had to stay separated from the people with the dead spirit cores to keep from killing them.

God's mere presence would cause the death of anyone with the sin nature. In Exodus, the people and priests were warned of God revealing His presence or "*breaking forth*" if they had not prepared properly to approach Him.

The purpose of the warning was to let them know that if they weren't right; God's very presence would kill them. What has *The* Cross done to and for us that we not only are not threatened by the presence of the Living God but have been invited into His inner circle? His presence is in us now. How is that for a reversal of misfortune?

2 Grace and peace be multiplied unto you through the knowledge of God, and of Jesus our Lord,
*3 According as his **divine** power has **given unto us** all things that pertain unto life and godliness, through the knowledge of him that has called us to glory and virtue:*
*4 Whereby are **given unto us** exceeding great and precious promises: that by these you might be partakers of **THE DIVINE NATURE**, having escaped the corruption that is in the world through lust.*   2 Peter 1:2-4

Take a close look at verse three above. Is it telling us that we partake of the divine nature through the knowledge of Him who rescued us? If so, where do we get that knowledge of Him? Through His Word right? Any wonder why the devil uses religion and false humility to convince people that the Bible tells us what is wrong with us? That is one reason we don't delve into the Bible like we should.

ACTUALLY, THE BIBLE TELLS THE NEW CREATION BELIEVER WHAT IS RIGHT WITH THEM. It tells the ungodly, wicked, and unrighteous what's wrong with them and the believer what is right with the believer. What is right with you. What is right with me. It is all in the grace mirror of God's Word. Look into it! Find the real you. **The righteous you.**

As we glean the truth of His love for us from His Word and accept that truth, we partake of more of His nature. His nature is in His word. The Word revelation of Him in us feeds our new spirit core with...Him? Can that be? Jesus did say that His blood is drink indeed and His flesh is food indeed. (John 6:55) You see, I don't have answers but I have a bit of a handle on asking the right questions. It does sound like feeding on the word of the Living God gives us the divine nature.

The divine nature. Is that the name of the new nature which evicted the old man from our spirit core? The divine nature in screwed up me? That sounded a bit blasphemous to me so I looked up that word in the Bible dictionary and one of the definitions is "godhead." How can that make sense that the Living God has offered part of His nature and shared it – given it actually – to former "wretches" like us? What do you call this much grace? More than _____.

If this is true then Jesus really pulled the short straw and got the worse end of the deal. He went through that Hell of suffering and separation from His Father God and we got invited into the inner circle? How can this be? Once we have the new nature (or at least seeds of the new nature) we are instructed to do something to make it grow. To make it better. To cause the roots to grow deep.

*5 And beside this, giving all diligence, **add to your** faith virtue; and to virtue knowledge;*
6 And to knowledge temperance; and to temperance patience; and to patience godliness;
7 And to godliness brotherly kindness; and to brotherly kindness charity.
*8 For **if** these things be in you, and abound, they make you that you shall neither be barren nor unfruitful in the knowledge of our Lord Jesus Christ.*   2 Peter 1:5-8

The Father gives us the measure of faith (Romans 12:3/Galatians 2:20) at salvation but we have to add these other spiritual dimensions to it. It is clear that we are fellow laborers with our Father (1ˢᵗ Corinthians 3:9) in the sanctification process. But don't gloat.

It is not our works which sanctify us but believing and receiving the benefits of Jesus' finished work which does the sanctifying. We get these dimensions from feeding on the spiritual flesh of the Lamb through the Word. His invitation to drink His blood and eat His flesh for spiritual life is completed in His word.

*5 **Mortify** therefore your members which are upon the earth; fornication, uncleanness, [**unnatural**] affection, [**shameful passion**], and covetousness, [**greed**] which is idolatry:*
6 For which things' sake the wrath of God cometh on the children of disobedience:
7 In the which you also walked some time, when you lived in them.
*8 But now you also **put off** all these; anger, wrath, malice, blasphemy, filthy communication out of your mouth.*
*9 **Lie not** one to another, seeing that you have put off the old man with his deeds;*
*10 And have **put on** the new man, which is renewed in knowledge after the image of him that created him:*
11 Where there is neither Greek nor Jew, [covenant members] nor [covenant outsiders],

Barbarian, Scythian, bond nor free: but Christ is all, and in all.

*12 **Put on** therefore, as the elect of God, holy and beloved, bowels of mercies, kindness, humbleness of mind, meekness, longsuffering;*

*13 **Forbearing** one another, and fo**rgiving** one another, if any man have a quarrel against any: even as Christ forgave you, so also do you.*

*14 And above all these things **put on** charity, which is the bond of perfectness.*

*15 And **let** the peace of God rule in your hearts, to the which also you are called in one body; and **be thankful**.*

*16 **Let** the word of Christ dwell in you richly in all wisdom; **teach**ing and **admonish**ing one another in psalms and hymns and spiritual songs, **sing**ing with grace in your hearts to the Lord.*

*17 And whatsoever you do in word or deed, do all in the name of the Lord Jesus, **giving thanks** to God and the Father by him.*   Colossians 3:5-17

Did you notice all of the action verbs in this passage? Those are our responsibility. Add, mortify, put off, put on, put away, let, forbear, forgive, and sin not. The act of the will is now firmly in our hands. *The* Cross has transformed our nature to the point that we now can "want to" do right and have the spiritual ability and help to do so.

So much of the transformation of justification has afforded us an active part in the sanctification of our souls. I call sanctification the process of the outside –our souls, minds, and bodies – catching up with the inside reality of our spirit core made in the image of our Savior according to 2nd Corinthians 3:18.

All of us, then, reflect the glory of the Lord with uncovered faces; and that same glory, coming from the Lord, who is the Spirit, transforms us into his likeness in an ever greater degree of glory.

2 Corinthians 3:18 TEV

No one was given this type of information under the Old Covenant because there was nothing they could do about the old man. The Law highlighted failings and shortcomings with no hope of doing anything about it. The devil was a mystery in the Old Testament because they had no authority over him. That is one reason Jesus said that the least person in the kingdom of God, the church, the body of Christ is greater than the greatest person and prophet of the Old Testament.(Matthew 11:11/Luke 7:28)   At the core, the spiritually dead belonged to the dark spirit. Any information about him would lead to hopelessness and maybe worse. Another reason Jesus made that statement was regarding the stark difference between **the Law** which **demanded righteousness** but couldn't empower it and **Grace** which **grants righteousness**.

People leading abominable lifestyles were wiped out because there was no transforming power to change the spirit core of humanity and give them the power of choice to "not let" sin dominate them. Protecting the bloodlines from disease was also a consideration. Seemingly benign behaviors were punished in ways we would consider overkill; but their system of conduct was behavioral modification. Punishment could contribute to that.

The spirit-core resurrecting power was far away. Also, particular diseases resulting from restricted behaviors could infect generations and potentially destroy entire civilizations and cultures. After the articles of war were announced in Eden (the seed of the woman will destroy the seed of the devil), the hellish strategy to contaminate bloodlines was put in motion.

*My dear children, I am writing this to you so that you will not sin. **But if** anyone does sin, we have an* *advocate who pleads our case before the Father. He is Jesus Christ, the one who is truly righteous.*

1 John 2:1 NLT

Awake to righteousness, and sin not...

1 Corinthians 15:34

After *The* Cross, though, sin is a choice based on 1st John 2:1. "You don't have to sin," Apostle John says, "but if you do; you have an advocate with the Father." Jesus is defending us even now. The accuser of the believers (Revelation 12:10) – our former father – accuses us day and night when we do wrong. When we fall. When we sin. John says that Jesus is our legal defender.

Even when we are clearly guilty, Jesus raises His hand to say, "I paid for that." 2nd Timothy 4:8 says that Christ is also *The Righteous Judge* who will put crowns of righteousness on us on His day.

24 But this man, because he continues ever, hath an unchangeable priesthood.
25 Wherefore he is able also to save them to the uttermost that come unto God by him, seeing he ever lives to make intercession for them.

Hebrews 7:24-25

Our righteous judge and legal defender is continually representing us in the unseen realm. In the court of Heaven. Do you understand now why we are strongly encouraged to come boldly to the throne of grace - *The* Cross - for mercy and grace? For mercy's sake, come!

We win on so many levels. Our Father loves us so much that He has made it so that all we do is win. (Romans 8:37; 2nd Corinthians 2:14) Even when the accuser is bringing charges against us day and night.(Revelation 12:10) This knowledge is supposed to give us the wherewithal to increase our desire and ability to sin less and eventually not at all. Religion, condemnation, and false humility teach, "when we sin" but the Word of God encourages, "IF we sin." Grace wins again!

The third chapter of Colossians teaches us that there is no race in the Kingdom of God. In the Kingdom of the Living God there is no Gentile or Jew. No class or religious privilege or even a difference in God's eyes between the slave and the master. If the Kingdom Spirit of Christ is in you then you are all the same in God's eyes. Still, Jesus takes this transformation to a whole new level when He combines them all in Himself. Hear what Paul says to the believers in Ephesus:

11 Wherefore remember, that you being in time past Gentiles in the flesh, who are called Uncircumcision [covenant outsiders] *by that which is called the Circumcision* [covenant insiders] *in the flesh made by hands;*

12 That at that time **you were without Christ**, being aliens from the commonwealth of Israel, and strangers from the covenants of promise, having no hope, and **without God** in the world:

13 But **now in Christ Jesus you** who sometimes were far off **are made nigh by the blood** of Christ.

14 For he is our peace, who has made both one, and has broken down the middle wall of partition between us;

15 Having abolished in his flesh the enmity, even the law of commandments contained in ordinances; for to **make in himself of two one new man**, so making peace;   [ONE NEW HUMANITY?]

16 And that he might reconcile both unto God in one body by the cross, having slain the enmity thereby:

17 And came and preached peace to you which were afar off, and to them that were nigh.

18 For through him we both have access by one Spirit unto the Father.

19 Now therefore you are no more strangers and foreigners, but fellow citizens with the saints, and of the household of God;

20 And are built upon the foundation of the apostles and prophets, Jesus Christ himself being the chief corner stone;

21 In whom all the building fitly framed together grows unto an holy temple in the Lord:

*22 In whom **you also are** built together for an **habitation of God** through the Spirit.*

Ephesians 2:11-22

Is *new humanity* another designation of the new nature we have because of *The* Cross? Dame Isabel Piczek's assertion that the resurrection created a new universe seems more feasible in light of this scripture. Jesus is the first born representative of a new human race? A race of born again humans? The blood of Christ called Gentiles into the inner circle of promise with Jews and then gave the new humanity a part in the divine nature of the Living God. This makes us fellow citizens in the kingdom of the Living God who has taken up residence in us through His Spirit.

How can this be?

The charis or grace of *The* Cross!

In light of this information, who do you think you are?

A wretched worm?

A sinner...saved by grace?   (doesn't exist)

A child of the Living God?

Dear friends, ***Now we are God's children NOW****; and it has not yet been made clear what we will become. We do know that when he appears, we will be like him; because we will see him as he really is.*   1 John 3:2 CJB

Once we become justified by faith in *The* Cross we are no longer called sinners. We are no more to be referred to as wretches. **Sinners and wretches** don't have a place in the divine nature. **Sinners and wretches** don't call the Living God who created the heavens, earth, and all that in them is Abba / Father. A sinner cannot address the LORD of creation as Daddy.   But believers can.

Sinners and wretches don't have the Kingdom Spirit residing within. You are either a saint or you aint. Rhyme over grammar? Good thing I am not a scholar. Religion attempts to guilt and trick us into mixing law (*sinner*) and grace (*saved by grace*) but the account of Ananias (means grace) and Sapphira (tablets of stone-law) in Acts chapter 5 tells us that mixing the two is fatal.

The letter to the Romans is amazing because it helps to explain the events of the unseen realm which transpired for our salvation. It offers the understanding of the sin nature as well as the spiritual identity and characteristics of the new creation believer. How would we understand justification without the clarion proclamation which Romans makes of justification?

Verse twenty six of chapter three declares the righteousness of Jesus, "*that [the Living God] might be just, and the justifier of those which believe in Jesus.*" We only have to offer faith in Jesus' cross and the Father exchanges it for justification. Sound like an offer we shouldn't refuse. Ephesians 2:8 says that God provides even the faith. We don't have to conjure our own faith. Simply accept it from Him.
WHOA!   AND   WOW!

How can anyone refuse that?   Still, some will.

Even those who say they do not. The religious who consciously and subconsciously alike view their religious duties, activities, and obligations as a method of accumulating grace or favors with God have their own system of works. Romans warns us that work and grace as objects of faith don't mix.

Now to him that works is the reward[of righteousness or justification] not reckoned of grace, but of debt.   Romans 4:4

Referring to Abraham's "acquisition" of righteousness in exchange for faith; this scripture tells us that IF he was declared righteous after completing specific tasks then the righteousness was owed to Abraham. On the other hand, if the righteousness is imputed immediately after faith is properly placed in the promises of God's Word; then is the imputation of righteousness a matter of graciousness and not wages earned. But that is not all. Listen to what the next verse says:

*But to him that [doesn't work for it], but believes on Him that **justifies the ungodly**, his faith is counted for righteousness.*   Romans 4:5

I use bold type because I want you to get it before I point it out. I have said in Bible study and worship settings, "If we simply slow down in our Bible reading we would get so much more out of it." If our primary focus during our Bible reading and study is to complete as many chapters and books as quickly as we can then we will miss so much of what we need to know to give us confidence on judgment day and peace in the midst of life's chaos.

Reading the Bible for volume over substance is turning what could be a nourishing meal into the equivalent of fast food. You may be satiated but not necessarily nourished. That being said, have you ever noticed something as exciting as this verse in your Bible reading? The Living God JUSTIFIES THE UNGODLY. I don't know how you feel about that but it gives me so much hope.

I don't know anything about being righteous, justified, holy, sanctified or feeling comfortable in and of myself when I think about judgment day. What I do know about is being ungodly. No one had to teach me that. What I do know about and am intimately acquainted with is being ungodly in my mind, thoughts, emotions, and motivations. When I consider that my sins were judged on Jesus' cross; that gives me confidence for judgment day.

I do know what it feels like to seem so screwed up that it absolutely amazes me that beyond any shadow of doubt I can say that I am a child of the Living God and have eternal life in my spirit core RIGHT NOW. Yes, right now although I don't "feel" saved. I don't "feel" righteous. I don't "feel" justified. I "feel" screwed up. I still "feel" like that proverbial Baptist wretch needs amazing grace to rescue me from eternal death. Thank God that **faith in the Word** of the Living God **has nothing to do with feelings**. It has to do with knowing. Yes, knowing.

*And this is life eternal, **that they might know** you the only true God, and Jesus Christ, whom thou hast sent.*   John 17:3

Just before Jesus' redemption suffering would commence; He prayed an amazing prayer for us all. He always gets His prayers answered because He knows how to pray right. You might want to visit the seventeenth chapter of John's gospel to get a broad picture of what He prayed for you. He also made some statements you can add faith to and claim for your situation.

*For **we know** that if our earthly house of this tabernacle were dissolved, we have a building of God, an house not made with hands, eternal in the heavens.*

2 For in this we groan, earnestly desiring to be clothed upon with our house which is from heaven: 2 Corinthians 5:1-2

*3 And hereby **we do know** that **we know him**, if we keep **his commandments**.*
4 He that says, I know him, and keeps not his commandments, is a liar, and the truth is not in him.
5 But whoso keeps his word, in him verily is the love of God perfected: hereby know we that we are in him.   1 John 2:3-5

Remember Jesus condensing all the commandments to love in the 22nd chapter of Matthew? The ten commands of behavior, intent, and motivation which the Living God gave Moses morphed into about 613 instructional do's and don'ts. Jesus said that having love for God and for people satisfies all the commandments. It takes faith to do that. Notice "His commandments" and "perfected love" seem to be synonymous?

He even makes it easy for us to keep His commandments. Being mindful of God's love inside us has to influence our behavior. Too much grace teaching will not result in lawless living. On the contrary, the knowledge of the charis of *The* Cross makes you want to live right; not to gain points but to make the Living Papa proud.

Beloved, **now** *are we the sons of God, and it doth not yet appear what we shall be: but* **we know** *that, when he shall appear, we shall be like him; for we shall see him as he is.* 1 John 3:2

And he that keeps his commandments dwells in him, and he in him. And hereby **we know** *that* **he abides in us, by the Spirit** *which he has given us.* 1 John 3:24

And we know that the Son of God is come, and has given us an understanding, **that we may know him** *that is true, and* **we are in him that is true***, even in his Son Jesus Christ. This is the true God, and eternal life.* 1 John 5:20

We know *that God's children do not make a practice of sinning,*[if the "want to" got saved] *for God's Son holds them securely, and the evil one cannot touch them.* 1 John 5:18 NLT

Being comfortable sinning after coming to Christ is a glaring indication of authentic salvation or not. This scripture in the original manuscript language paints an encouraging picture. It teaches that the new creation believer cannot produce sin from the inside out. What does that mean? The resurrected spirit core does not produce or create sin as the dead spirit core did previously. That is encouraging to know that IF I do sin, it is the old man residue in the soul, mind, and body and not the real me. Not the new me. **The new you doesn't sin directly because it [your spirit] is born of the Living God.** Such good news. Condemnation be damned! Just remember to cooperate with the Almighty through His Word, His Spirit, and prayer.

That is encouraging. However, sexual immorality was on every short list of discipleship instructions that James and the other apostles gave to new converts. The apostles did not want to burden the new believers with a bunch of commandments. Some teachers were tempted to direct new believers to follow the Law. However, the *apostles of grace* gave few restrictions. Sexual immorality was one. Sexual encounters fuse souls together (Genesis 2:24/Mark 10:8). The new creation believer has had the spirit core fused to Christ. The soul begins the sanctification process. Sexual immorality is not good for sanctification. It is not good for anything or anyone.

The new believer and the long-time church member alike have to be taught about the sanctification process. What the traditional church has done is given a laundry list of don'ts while, in many cases, not listing the do's. We didn't explain the transition between knowing what not to do and what to do and how to feel if you find yourself doing what you shouldn't be doing.

Suffice it to say that if you are as comfortable sinning now as you were before Christ then you should come to Christ again and find a good book on the subject of sanctification as well as a person you can confide in to talk to about sanctification. If you are comfortable exhibiting the works of the flesh then you may need to revisit the foot of *The* Cross.

9 And be found in him, not having mine own righteousness, which is of the law, but that which is through the faith of Christ, the righteousness which is of God by faith:
*10 That **I may know him, and** [know] the power of his resurrection, **and** [know] the fellowship of his sufferings, being made conformable unto his death;* Philippians 3:9-10

My own righteousness which is by the law? The righteousness which is by religion? Religion is the practice of approaching God based on your own performance and assumptions. Cain approached the Most High God based on Cain's assumptions rather than the Most High's instructions. The result was Cain's worship being rejected. Abel approached the Most High the way the Most High instructed and Abel's worship was accepted. Faith in the grace of *The* Cross means approaching the throne of grace based on Jesus' performance and not our own.

That I may know Him, and know Him, and know Him? You see, the righteousness, which is the result of faith in what Jesus did for us results in a confidence to know Him and to know more and more about Him. On the other hand, the righteousness, which comes from works, results in uncertainty. Have I done enough? Have I dotted all the I's and crossed all the t's? I don't understand the Hebrew alephbet well enough to add some clever thought about dotting the I's but I will suggest that Jesus crossed all the t's for us – with His cross. The only thing left for us to do is put faith in it and walk in love. In Almighty God's agape love because faith works by love according to Galatians 5:6. Our Loving Father has made faith so simple. Just believe in the love our Father has for us and accept His promises.

JESUS' CROSS SPEAKS TO A CONCLUSION which cannot be argued: the Living God loves us to much to leave us the way we are. Humanity needed to be rescued and had no hope of rescuing itself. Jesus' offer of unearned righteousness is a glaring neon sign letting us know that we could never work enough to be good enough or righteous enough to know Him the way He wants to know us and the way He wants us to know Him. So, we just need to give up our own dead works [religion, good deeds, ulterior charity, duplicitous generosity], inaccurate perceptions, and hellish condemnation and accept His righteousness which only comes through faith in *The* Cross.

The love walk is an act of faith. A lifestyle of faith. If we truly believe what the Word says about the love of the Living God being put inside us (Romans 5:5) then that means we have the capacity to be more loving than we are now. As we walk in it, it is not the love capacity which increases but our expression and understanding of it that does. No matter how loving you are or are not; you can be more loving. I know I can. Just as His spirit is living in us; He wants His love to flow out of us.

The word of the Living God says that we can have confidence that we are His children and face eternity with peace of spirit and mind because of Jesus' cross. We can KNOW that we are His children regardless of how we feel about ourselves. We feel screwed up because we know what trash is in our heart, mind, and thoughts. But that trash is actually residue of the sin nature in our souls, minds, and bodies. Even while we are in the process of becoming, He still uses us for His glory and the benefit of others.

Yes, the Holy Spirit only resides in perfect people so how can he be in me, in you, in us as screwed up as we are? Could it be because of Jesus' perfection being on loan to us? In light of what we've learned so far; shouldn't that be, "as screwed up as we *think* we are?" That question will be answered soon and convincingly; but we have to settle the issue that it is our soul and body which struggle with behaviors of the sinful past.

The change has to be deeper than the soul. Down in the spirit core where faith is. Where we can believe the Word and know; just know that we are right with the Living God. Not because of anything that we've done; but because of EVERYTHING that He's done. 1st Thessalonians 5:23 answers clearly that Christ's

GERALD MCCRAY

redemption work was completed in the spirit core. The rest of the human construct – the soul and body – are yet to be redeemed.

Yes, the "*knowing*" which trumps the feeling comes from faith in what the Living God has said. At creation He said, "Light be!" And light was and still is. What do you think happens when He calls the ungodly which puts faith in *The* Cross, "justified," "redeemed," "my child?" Has the light gone out yet?   Connect the dots.

In Genesis chapter one, we see that the sun was created on the fourth day while the light was created on day one. According to the twenty-first and twenty-second chapters of Revelation, the light will never go out. He does not unmake or unname. He made you righteous. He made you His child. He made you justified.

There are lyrics in a particular church song which say, "*I have a new name over in Glory and it's mine, mine, mine.*"   No, *The* Cross has given you a new name over here.   Many names. And they are yours, yours, yours.   One of your new names is **Redeemed**.

Another is **Justified**.
Another is **Sanctified**.
Another is **Heir** of the Living God.
Another is **Joint Heir** with Jesus.

The sun will no longer be needed because the light will continue to shine. Condemnation is no longer your concern because justification, righteousness, and redemption will continue forever. (Ephesians 2:7) Look at Genesis again and see that the Living God created the sun after He created the light. Wow!

So, all I have to do to get right with the Living God is to simply believe (put faith) in the word of the Living God which tells me that *Jesus who was not acquainted with sin was made to be sin for us [ME - YOU so] that we [I - YOU] might be made the righteousness of God in HIM.* (2 Corinthians 5:21)

Yes, in Him! We must be in Him to be newly named.   The reason multitudes will reject *The* Cross is because it is too easy. There is no effort. There is no sense of accomplishment. Some will be too proud to accept God's charity. I just believe in it and receive the benefits of the same. The ungodly – those without God – can instantaneously be transformed to children of the Living God by simply putting faith in Jesus' cross? That is one reason that grace has been described as amazing.   **We can face judgment based on our performance or on Jesus' performance**. Since He passed the test already; let's go with His.   Yes Jesus, Yes!

CHAPTER THREE

SPIRIT SOUL AND BODY

Now may the God of peace Himself sanctify you completely; and may your whole spirit, soul, and body be preserved blameless at the coming of our Lord Jesus Christ.

1 Thessalonians 5:23

The original chapter title for this discussion is *Sanctification: What The Cross Does In Us.* The cross in us? If you have been any time in churches or organized religion you are probably thinking, "I thought it is the Holy Spirit in us," and you would be right but the only reason God's Spirit can take up residence in broken humanity is because of *The* Cross which scrubs us clean. So much so that the Holy Spirit can make our resurrected spirit core His new temple according to 1st Corinthians 3:2, 3:16-17, 6:19, 2nd Corinthians 6:16, and 1st Peter 2:5.

*For by one offering **he has perfected for ever** them that are sanctified.*   Hebrews 10:14

Listen to John's gospel on the then to come indwelling of the Holy Spirit in the new creation believer. Jesus promises the indwelling, prays for the indwelling, and prays for us to understand the love of the Father and just how much the Living Father will and has invested in us and has deposited in us.

16 And I will ask the Father, and he will give you another Counselor to be with you forever—
*17 **the Spirit of truth**. The world cannot accept him, because it neither sees him nor knows him. But you know him, for he lives with you and **will be in you**.*   John 14:16-17 NIV

*12 "I have much more to say to you, **more than you can now bear**.*
13 But when he, the Spirit of truth, comes, he will guide you into all truth. He will not speak on his own; he will speak only what he hears, and he will tell you what is yet to come.
14 He will bring glory to me by taking from what is mine and making it known to you.

John 16:12-14 NIV

24 "Father, I want those you have given me to be with me where I am, and to see my glory, the glory you have given me because you loved me before the creation of the world.
25 "Righteous Father, though the world does not know you, I know you, and they know that you have sent me.
*26 I have made you known to them, and will continue to make you known in order that the love you have for me may be in them and that **I MYSELF MAY BE IN THEM**."* John 17:24-26 NIV

One of the most important of the additional things which Jesus said that we were not able to bear or understand had to be the fact that He Himself would take up residence in the spirit core of the new creation believer. The great thing about the promise from the Father in John 16 is that the Holy Spirit will continue the teaching which Jesus couldn't share at the time. And the Holy Spirit will teach us from the inside out making it easier for us to receive and accept it maybe.

Is it possible that He takes up residence in us because we are no longer broken...at the core I mean? On the Day of Pentecost, the Holy Spirit came and filled everyone in the Upper Room. Their meeting spilled out into the streets where Peter preached a spirit filled and spirit flowing message and more than three thousand people from many parts of the world came to faith in Jesus' cross and was filled with the Holy Spirit. Guess what? The second chapter of Acts recounts the first recorded incidents of the Holy Spirit filling people compared to coming upon them as is cited in the Old Testament. Even Mary of Nazareth had the Holy Spirit come upon her to conceive Messiah Jesus. The Upper Room prayer group, which included Mary, was indwelt first and then the more than three thousand of those making the annual pilgrimage to Jerusalem.

HERE'S AN INTERESTING STATEMENT: Jesus wasn't filled with the Holy Spirit like the believers were in the second chapter of Acts. With the Virgin Mary in the mix; He was born of the Spirit like new creation believers are.

Because He came back from spiritual death; He was reborn like new creation believers are. Jesus was an Old Testament prophet and thus operated as they did. I know that statement initially sounds heretical and blasphemous to the religious mind but let us reason together before you reject it out of hand.

The Day of Pentecost in the second chapter of the book of Acts is the first time the Holy Spirit began His indwelling ministry to the believer. Under the old covenant, the Holy Spirit rested upon or covered individuals. Because Jesus was modeling the ministry for us; He operated in the same vane as the other Old Testament prophets.

The Son of God worked as a prophet under the Old Covenant and thus used the same tools they had at their disposal. His perfect Spirit Core was the difference. Now, His Spirit has taken up residence in our spirit core. (John 17:26)

Listen to what Jesus says about Himself after He returns to His home town of Nazareth from His wilderness temptation in the fourth chapter of Luke's gospel; and contrast that with what the Living Father's Word says about **the anointing which He deposited IN US** according to 1st John 2:27.

*18 The Spirit of the Lord is **upon** me, because he has anointed me to preach the gospel to the poor;*

he has sent me to heal the brokenhearted, to preach deliverance to the captives, and recovering of sight to the blind, to set at liberty them that are bruised,

19 To preach the acceptable year of the Lord.

20 And he closed the book, and he gave it again to the minister, and sat down. And the eyes of all them that were in the synagogue were fastened on him.

21 And he began to say unto them, This day is this scripture fulfilled in your ears. Luke 4:18-21

For The New Creation Believer:

*As for you, **the anointing** you received from him **remains in you**, and you do not need anyone to teach you. But as his anointing teaches you about all things and as that anointing is real, not counterfeit; just as it has taught you, remain in him.* 1 John 2:27 NIV

Before Jesus departs for His appointment with *The* Cross, He tells His disciples that the Holy Spirit will reside inside them. That wasn't the case in the Old Testament and Jesus as an Old Testament prophet operated in ministry in the same manner as the other Old Testament prophets. Why is that distinction important? Please keep in mind that if Jesus was living His life and performing His ministry as the Son of God and then asks us to follow in His footsteps then that would be totally unfair. How could broken humanity walk the way God walked on this earth? In summarizing Jesus' life many years after His ascension, Peter says this about Him in Peter's second letter to the church at large:

21 For even hereunto were you called: because Christ also suffered for us, leaving us an example, that you should follow his steps:
22 Who did no sin, neither was guile found in his mouth:
23 Who, when he was despised, despised not again; when he suffered, he threatened not; but committed himself to him that judges righteously:
1 Peter 2:21-23

No guile found in His mouth? That Greek word translated guile has multiple meanings such as:

decoy	trick	bait	
wile	craft	deceit	subtlety[ii]

All of these terms can be summed up with one word – deception. Maybe even "lies." From car dealerships baiting and switching shoppers to unethical politicians parsing the meaning of the word "is;" when people use subtle deception we simply call it lying. Not only was Jesus not a liar but He was so committed to truth that He didn't parse words or defraud anyone in the slightest way. He is the truth! (John 14:6) And this Jesus said of Himself that the Holy Spirit was upon Him not in Him. Yes, He was reading and quoting the prophet Isaiah but keep in mind that Isaiah was prophesying about the future Messiah. Isaiah was talking about the Christ.

When He took up residence in our resurrected spirit cores; all of His character traits came with Him. All of His anointing came with Him as well. All of His peace. All of His calm. All of His anointing...maybe? Maybe all in seed form considering that seeding, time, and harvest is a process of first mention in the book of beginnings – Genesis. In seed form means that we have the potential for so much more but it has to be cultivated and nourished to grow or expand.

Just as scientists have concluded that the universe is still expanding[iii] (since the Living God said, "Light be!") [from that single boson/fermion seed maybe?] after thousands of years; the seed of the divine nature will expand in us as we water it with the Word of God as well as with proper words coming from our mouths.

Bosons and fermions? I don't pretend to know in detail what I am referring to but my awareness of the concepts has been enhanced by a series of lectures. Still, what do they have to do with Jesus' cross? Suffice it to say that I am a big fan of both the Big Bang Theory sitcom and Brad Scott's WildBranch Ministry teaching on the Hebraic Roots Network. The explanations of the intricacies of the Hebrew alephbet's impact on DNA and the fundamental elements of creation are simply amazing.

Under the Old Covenant, the relationship certain people had with God included the benefit of the Holy Spirit helping them complete the tasks given them by God. He came down upon one prophet and caused him to overtake and outrun a horse. (1st Kings 18:44-46) The anointing remained upon a prophet's skeleton for years causing a corpse being lowered into the same tomb to revive after coming into contact with it. The anointing, which was upon Jesus, is now inside the new creation believers' spirit core. Is that the root of the greater works potential which each new creation believer has?

Here are a few scripture references describing the interaction of God's Spirit being "upon" the Old Testament believers and not working or dwelling within:

Numbers 11:29   Isaiah 42:1, 44:3

Ezekiel 39:29   Joel 2:28

Matthew 12:18   Acts 2:17

The Spirit of God whether upon broken humanity or dwelling within broken humanity is quite something so don't get me wrong. When God has wonders to perform, He will do it His way and He will do it wonderfully. I am simply making a point about the footsteps of Jesus and the amazing feat accomplished by His cross. His cross made it possible for broken humanity to have God's Spirit DWELLING INSIDE BELIEVERS forever. How can that be? Is it possible that the new creation believer is no longer broken at the spirit core? Can that be true?

Even the most devout believer has not mastered a life that is free of deceit and subtlety; and yet the Holy Spirit of God dwells within. That has to make you think of how amazing His grace is. You might sometimes think of yourself as a walking trashcan because of your familiarity with the darkness deep down inside. And sometimes right under the surface. Still, the Word says that as a new creation believer; the Spirit of the Living God resides within according to Colossians 1:27 and 1st Corinthians 6:19.

We know God cannot lie (Titus 1:2) so what He says about us has to be true. That means that the Living God's best work wasn't done through perfect Jesus but is done through "screwed up" us. We are only screwed up in our souls and bodies until they are transformed using the Word of God. In our resurrected spirit core, we are perfect because of Jesus' blood.(Ephesians 4:24/Hebrews 10:14/12:23) I think one reason why church people don't read their Bibles as much as they should is because they expect to find more of what's wrong with them in the pages. On the contrary, the Living God has loaded His word with life transforming information.

I recently heard a lecturer say that the word *information* comes from a Greek word which means "to give life." I looked up the word and found that one definition is "to animate," or breathe life. Life giving information from the life giving Word of the Living God? Grace, grace, grace, and more grace!

So, take the information found in the Word and make it yours first and foremost by receiving it. No, really! Actually say, "Father, I receive your

Word calling me the righteousness of God in Christ Jesus and I ask you to help me believe it and own it." You can use that example for all of His promises. Keep in mind that some of the promises in His Word are conditional [where the "if" is apparent or implied] so govern yourself accordingly. Imagine how effective praying His Word back to Him is.

Also, it is extremely important to make the point that just because a new creation believer is guilty of behavior unbecoming the family of the Living God; that doesn't mean that the individual is a fake or fraud. The biggest challenge all of us have in cooperating with the Spirit of our Heavenly Father is that the old nature residue remains in the soul, mind, emotions, and body and can be enticed by the lust of the eyes, the lust of the flesh, and the pride of life (1st John 2:16) which won't be eradicated until the perfect incorruptible outside [soul and body] replaces the current outside.

53 For this corruptible must put on incorruption, and this mortal must put on immortality.
*54 So **when** this corruptible shall have put on incorruption, and this mortal shall have put on immortality, **then** shall be brought to pass the saying that is written, Death is swallowed up in*

victory.

55 O death, where is thy sting? O grave, where is thy victory?   1 Corinthians 15:53-55

15 Love not the world, neither the things that are in the world. If any man love the world, the love of the Father is not in him.

*16 For all that is in the world, **the lust of the flesh**, and **the lust of the eyes**, and **the pride of life**, is not of the Father, but is of the world.*

17 And the world passes away, and the lust thereof: but he that doeth the will of God abides forever.   1 John 2:15-17

*[The Kingdom Spirit of the Living God] is a deposit guaranteeing our inheritance until the redemption of **[the bodies and souls]** those who are God's possession — to the praise of his glory.*
                    Ephesians 1:14 NIV

The Holy Spirit taking up residence in the spirit core of the new creation believer is called an earnest deposit of our inheritance from our Father God. Earnest money in a contract transaction is a *"good faith"* guarantee that the transaction will be completed. All of what Jesus' cross did for us is simply a deposit. Earnest money is the smallest part of a property transaction. If it is the same with this spiritual transaction which justified and sanctified us; can you imagine what the completion of this transaction will entail? Imagine!

9 But as it is written, Eye has not seen, nor ear heard, neither have entered into the heart of man, the things which God has prepared for them that love him.
10 But God has revealed them unto us by his Spirit: for the Spirit searches all things, yea, the deep things of God.   1 Corinthians 2:9-10

The soul and body, outside of the resurrected spirit core, can be triggered by and tugged on by what dominated it before salvation. The lust of the flesh, lust of the eyes, and the pride of life came with the sin nature which Adam introduced into the world. Adam's actions also introduced the sin nature into the human spirit and it has gained momentum ever since.

Still, they don't have to dominate if we are careful to keep the mirror of God's Word top of mind. That is why John adds to his epistle, "If we sin," in 1st John 2:1 rather than, "when we sin." That point cannot be taken lightly. John is teaching that falling and sinning don't have to happen but IF they do; our advocate continues advocating on our behalf.

Absolutely amazing grace!

What's more is how the 1st chapter of John's epistle ended.

8 If we say that we have no sin, we deceive ourselves, and the truth is not in us.
*9 **If** we confess our sins, he is faithful and just to forgive us our sins, and to cleanse us from all unrighteousness.*
10 If we say that we have not sinned, we make him a liar, and his word is not in us.   1 John 1:8-10

The journey we are on right now is going to include some exciting revelation stations along the way. Our destination will conclude with a clear but mind blowing understanding of what makes grace so amazing. This 1st chapter of 1st John has some information for us which we cannot simply brush over. The Word opens this second chapter with the understanding that we don't have to sin. It is absolutely liberating to learn that **the dark spirit cannot make you do anything**. You have a choice. You can cooperate with the Living God or you can cooperate with the dark spirit. But the dark spirit cannot make you do anything once you are God's child.

The sixth chapter of the letter to the Romans calls cooperating with the Living God yielding our members to righteousness. Obviously, cooperating with the dark spirit – sin – is lending our members to unrighteousness. That realization makes the epistle of 1st John critically important to our spiritual journey. In chapter two of *Whatever Happened To The Cross?* I asserted that the most important word in the Bible is "if" and 1st John is confirming that statement in regard to repentance. The understanding that *The* Cross justifies us [faith in His cross] doesn't stop us from sinning. The liberating information of sanctification doesn't make the sinning stop either. BUT understanding the provisions our Heavenly Father has put in place to get us back on track keeps us from getting stuck in the mud of condemnation. It also has us slowing down to consider the consequences of our potential actions; and may cause us not to act at all. Grace!

*1 For **the law** having a shadow of good things to come, and not the very image of the things, **can never** with those sacrifices which they offered year by year continually make **[those offering sacrifices]** perfect.*

GERALD McCRAY

2 For then would they not have ceased to be offered? because that the worshippers once purged should have had no more [sin consciousness].
3 But in those sacrifices there is a remembrance again made of sins every year. Hebrews 10:1-3

The failure of the Old Covenant sacrificial system is that sin consciousness could not be dealt with. The people had to be reminded of sin annually as a nation. That mentality haunted them every day. They left the sacrificial ceremony considering next year when they would have to return. The letter to the Hebrews opens up with the subject of the superiority of Yeshua Jesus over angel worship. Later, the superiority of Jesus as the final sacrifice of the law is expounded to a masterful crescendo. The most significant benefit of Jesus' sacrifice compared to the hundreds of thousands if not millions of Old Testament sacrifices is Jesus' sacrifice washes the conscience as well as the spirit. Not only are we cleansed and our sins forgiven but the condemnation and shame is washed away as well. Condemnation has no place in the life or mind of the new creation believer.

We don't have to spin our wheels in sin

consciousness, regret, condemnation, and shame. The hamster wheel of condemnation gets us nowhere. There is absolutely no progress there. We can get moving again by owning it, apologizing to our Heavenly Father for it, and He does the rest. He cleanses us from all unrighteousness. **IF** we do sin, we can get cleansed from that sin and from that unrighteousness IF we confess the sin. Some of the antiquated study helps which I used twenty years ago offered one of the definitions for the word "confess" as regurgitate. Vomit? Repenting of and confessing wrongdoing is a spiritual cleansing. We must confess to get it out of us. We must confess to get cleansed by the blood of Jesus' cross and once He washes away ALL unrighteousness; what do you think is left over? If all unrighteousness is washed away then the only thing left is righteousness. We must confess it to avoid becoming comfortable sinning. Do you see how amazingly His grace helps us get back up again?

If we refuse to allow the dark spirit to beat us down with condemnation and shame; then there is nothing it can do with us. We can always KNOW (versus feeling) that our conscience is cleansed because of *The* Cross. In 2nd Corinthians 7:2, the Apostle Paul says, "we wronged no man."

Isn't this the same person who dragged Christians back to Jerusalem to be executed for following and preaching that Jesus is the Messiah? Actually, no it isn't. The man which killed followers of *The Way* was Saul of Tarsus who met Yeshua Jesus while he was headed to Damascus to find more Christians to kill. The man Saul died in that meeting with Christ and was reborn the Apostle Paul. Because the blood of Jesus' cross cleanses the mind as well as the spirit; Paul could honestly and truthfully say that he wronged no one. That is a perfect example of Jesus' blood annihilating sin consciousness. Wow!

Well, what if I get caught up in unrighteousness ten times for the same thing? Then confess it to Him each time after running boldly to the throne of grace – *The* Cross. It is on purpose that the Word encourages us to come to the throne of grace boldly because He is anxious to forgive us and get us going on our journey again. I call Jesus' cross the throne of grace but that doesn't mean I am correct. I say that because I am convinced that the same cross which rescues the sinner sanctifies the saint.

We were made the justified children of our Living Father God by *The* Cross; were we not? **That same cross which justifies the ungodly**

sanctifies the saint. It makes sinners saints and saints sanctified. The ungodly justified and the justified the righteousness of God IN CHRIST. It is so hard not to scream, "Glory!" Speaking of glory; that same cross deposited the glory of God [divine nature?] inside us. His amazing grace pulls us from the dead, gives us life, and constantly washes us (1st John 1:17) IF we follow His prescription.

Justification picks us up out of our spiritual graves – dead in sin – and sanctification puts us back together.

In Ezekiel's vision of the valley of sun dried bones; the future inner dwelling of the Holy Spirit is promised after what sounds like some resurrection event of the old covenant people as a nation.

11 Then he said unto me, Son of man, these bones are the whole house of Israel: behold, they say, Our bones are dried, and our hope is lost: we are cut off for our parts.

12 Therefore prophesy and say unto them, Thus says the Lord God; Behold, O my people, I will open your graves, and cause you to come up out of your graves, and bring you into the land of Israel.

13 And you shall know that I am the Lord, **when I have opened your graves***, O my people, and*

brought you up out of your graves,
*14 And **shall put my spirit in you**, and you shall*
live, and I shall place you in your own land: then
shall you know that I the Lord have spoken it, and
performed it, says the Lord.   Ezekiel 37:11-14

There is an amazing promise in Joel's prophecy which points to some significant Holy Spirit interaction with humanity as a whole that may sound a bit blasphemous initially but one of the promises in the list of scriptures above is also found in the prophet Joel's proclamation.

Not just upon God's helpers and God's people but Joel prophesizes that Most High God promises to pour out His Holy Spirit **UPON ALL FLESH**. I know that scholars don't use all caps and bold type but I am not a scholar. I like to make my points clearly.

27 And you shall know that I am in the midst of Israel, and that I am the Lord your God, and none else: and my people shall never be ashamed.
*28 And it shall come to pass afterward, that I will pour out **my spirit upon all flesh**; and your sons and your daughters shall prophesy, your old men shall dream dreams, your young men shall see visions:*
29 And also upon the servants and upon the

handmaids in those days will I pour out my spirit.
30 And I will show wonders in the heavens and in
the earth, blood, and fire, and pillars of smoke.
31 The sun shall be turned into darkness, and the
moon into blood, before the great and the terrible
day of the Lord come.
32 And it shall come to pass, that whosoever shall
call on the name of the Lord shall be delivered: for
in mount Zion and in Jerusalem shall be
deliverance, as the Lord has said, and in the
remnant whom the Lord shall call. Joel 2:27-32

It is understandable that those with the covenant mentality would conclude that the "all flesh" promise meant all covenant flesh but that is not what is being communicated here. He even mentions pouring out His Spirit on the slaves and servants. The Jews had servants and slaves if they had the means and in most cases the slaves were not fellow Jews but foreigners. The Living God is promising to pour our His Holy Spirit on foreigners as well. I understand if someone refuses to accept that but the promise is worded in a way that gives the Living God the latitude to pour out His Spirit on anybody. Saved or not. Christian or not. Jewish or not. It is mind blowing to think just how far reaching the power of the cross extends.

Keep in mind that "upon" is not salvation. Maybe the entire universe, as postulated by Dame Isabel Piczek, was recreated by the power of Jesus' resurrection. Now I understand why thousands of Moslems are dreaming about Jesus and coming to faith in His cross. Let me explain.

I was watching a show on Christian television one day and this lady tells about how she dreamt of the same man for over forty years having no idea who He was.

One day someone came to her business telling her about Jesus. Over the course of the conversation the lady says, "I met Him in my dreams. Why have I been dreaming about Jesus for the last 40 years?" The "missionary" says to her, ["Because Jesus loves you enough to have died for your sins on the cross."] If memory serves, this lady came to faith in Jesus' cross immediately. I was actually channel surfing quite some time ago when I came across this testimony so precision is not clear. The host or reporter of this segment said, "These types of dreams have been reported in multiple Moslem cultures." Once these people had some type of explanation of their dreams they eventually came to faith in *The* Cross as well.

What an amazing testimony of the Living God's Agape Love. I wanted to confirm that statement about Moslems dreaming about Jesus so I went online and searched "Moslems dreaming about Jesus," and found that the politically correct/public relations spelling – "Muslims" – is the only search option. I also found real life evidence of Joel's prophesy in action. I watched so many testimonies of *the man Christ Jesus* (1st Timothy 2:5) introducing Himself to the Moslem people in dreams, visions, and the like. Jesus' cross not only opened the door of the spirit core for the indwelling of God's Spirit inside the believer but for the Holy Spirit to be poured out upon all flesh for the glory of God and the rescue of broken humanity.

In the twenty-first chapter of Genesis, the Living God told Hagar, mother of Ismail [Islam?], that He would take care of the boy [because he did come from Abraham's bloodline.] Abraham started an Hebrew-Egyptian bloodline with Ismail through Hagar/Hajar. He also started an Israeli/Arab bloodline through his third wife named Keturah. Some Rabbinical scholars postulate that Hagar and Keturah are the same person. Every bloodline which is a product of Abraham's reproductive activities will be chased down and invited into the charis (grace) of *The* Cross because our Living Father keeps His promises to a thousand generations (Deut. 7:9) which emblematically means "forever." Since it is not the Living God's will that any person be lost (2nd Peter 3:9) forever; He is definitely going after the descendants of Abraham. According to Jesus' teaching in John 8:31-59 as well as Hebrews 11: 4, 1st John 3:11-13, and Jude 1:10-15; one's religious and or spiritual allegiance indicates who their actual spiritual father is.

What a mighty and marvelous Living God we serve who sends His Spirit to draw people to *The* Cross which saves the sinner and sanctifies the believer. If the spirit core of the believer has been reconnected to the Spirit of the Living God; then sanctification must be the method or process of the two other parts of the human construct, the soul and body, catching up with or coming into alignment with the new spirit core.

So, what is the sanctifying process? Many years ago, I heard some Bible teacher say, "If you let Him, the Holy Spirit will live the Christian life through you and you end up getting the credit in the end." I don't know how accurate that is but I think it may be in line with the conclusion that our spirit cores are reconnected to the Spirit of the Living God at salvation. Jesus wanted the Holy Spirit inside the believer for a reason. Maybe it is the sanctification process. And maybe that is merely the beginning. As mentioned earlier, there are some information nuggets which we received under the New Covenant which we don't see in the Old Testament. We are told of the devil maybe sixty times in the New Testament but that title is not mentioned once in the Old Testament. We are warned of devils/demons over fifty times but they are mentioned about five times in the Old Testament. We are schooled on our choice over the sin nature but the Old Testament saints focused on avoiding superficial sinful behaviors.

For sin shall [no longer] exert dominion over you, since now you are not under Law [as slaves], but under grace [as subjects of God's favor and mercy]. Romans 6:14 AMP

You see that? You will no longer be dominated by sin. Sin dominated before the cross and that is why the sin nature was never heard of in the Old Testament. Yes, sin was dealt with but on a superficial level compared to an at-the-core transformation.

To be clear, though, the *sin nature* is not a term you will find in the Bible but as you read the Bible regarding the nature of sin and the consequence of Adam's sin being passed on to all who came after him; you will easily agree that human nature has been tainted by sin. We can connect the dots to come to a well founded and accurate conclusion that the sin nature is what Jesus' cross deals with.

The above scripture from Romans 6:14 is a glimpse into the sin nature which is explored in depth in the book of Romans and especially the 6th chapter. This verse gives a startling clue into the impact sin has on the unbeliever – dominion. A famous black male comedian, while in character as a woman, blamed "her" bad behavior on the devil during those memorable skits. "The devil made me do it," was the character's tag line which the audience looked forward to hearing every time the show aired. The sin nature was the puppeteer and we were the marionettes tethered to its whims. That was the lot of all humanity before *The* Cross of Christ.

There was some truth to Geraldine's popular statement, though. It wasn't the devil per se but the nature of the serpent [remember Moses' bronze snake discussion?] or the spiritually dead human spirit core which strongly influenced bad behavior, intentions, and emotions. There also an exciting statement in the seventh chapter of Romans right after the sixth chapter detailed what could easily be considered hopelessness in regard to the sin nature. Romans 7:5 says, "When we were in the flesh...," the results of our actions were death. When we were in the flesh? The person who was used by the Spirit to write Romans still had a natural body at the time so what does that mean? Wouldn't you know it? The eighth chapter of Romans has the answer.

*9 But you are not in the flesh, but in the Spirit, **if** so be that the Spirit of God dwells in you. Now **if** any man has not the Spirit of Christ, he is none of his.*
*10 And **if** Christ be in you, the body is dead because of sin; but the Spirit is life because of righteousness.*   Romans 8:9-10

WOW! But wait! There is so much more. Backing up to the first two verses of Romans chapter eight we see that the indwelling of the Spirit of God in the spirit core of the new creation believer results in the lack of condemnation. His word does not say that you are in the Spirit if you have dotted all the i's and crossed all the t's. The Living God says that you are in the Spirit **IF His Spirit resides in you**. You are not in the Spirit if you don't sin, stumble, fall, or fail but **IF His Spirit resides in you.** If His Spirit resides in me then how can I sin, stumble, fall, or fail? I can't wait!

Backing up a bit farther to the closing verses

of Romans chapter seven we see Paul voicing the struggles we all have. He even says that the struggle between knowing what to do and actually accomplishing it is like our spirit dragging around a dead body on our backs. After *The* Cross completed what it was supposed to for us New Covenant believers; we are informed by Romans 6:12 that, "sin will no more dominate you," [if you accept what Jesus did for you on the cross.]

Romans, 1st John, and Ephesians implores us to, "not sin." If we had no ability or newly formed capacity to not sin then it would be unfair, unjust, and maniacal to command us in such a way. We must then conclude that we do have a new capacity. We simply need to learn how to keep the old nature from dominating us like before. Dominate? Yes dominate like a slave master.

Before faith in *The* Cross transforms **the broken** into **the fixed** we are dominated by sin. We are slaves to it and have no chance of escaping the sin plantation because the sin plantation of the soul follows you everywhere you go and influences everything you do. Even good things. Even religious things. Listen to how Jesus berated the most religiously devout leaders of Israel:

Pretentious Prayers

37 A large crowd was listening to Jesus gladly.

38 As he taught them, he said, "Watch out for the teachers of the Law, who like to walk around in their long robes and be greeted with respect in the marketplace,

39 who choose the reserved seats in the synagogues and the best places at feasts.

40 They take advantage of widows and rob them of their homes, and then make a show of saying long prayers. Their punishment will be all the worse!" Mark 12:37-40 TEV

Religious Activity Void of God's Spirit

27 "What sorrow awaits you teachers of religious law and you Pharisees. Hypocrites! For you are like whitewashed tombs—beautiful on the outside but filled on the inside with dead people's bones and all sorts of impurity.

28 Outwardly you look like righteous people, but inwardly your hearts are filled with hypocrisy and lawlessness. Matthew 23:27-28 NLT

Endorsing Behavior Contrary to God's Instructions

8 For you ignore God's specific orders and substitute your own traditions.

9 You are simply rejecting God's laws and

trampling them under your feet for the sake of tradition.

10 For instance, Moses gave you this law from God: 'Honor your father and mother.' And he said that anyone who speaks against his father or mother must die.

11 But you say it is perfectly all right for a man to disregard his needy parents, telling them, 'Sorry, I can't help you! For I have given to God what I could have given to you.'

12-13 And so you break the law of God in order to protect your man-made tradition. And this is only one example. There are many, many others."

Mark 7:8-13 TLB

What about those "Christian" denominations which brazenly ordain and put on display leaders who unrepentantly encourage lifestyles which the Living God has clearly called abominable? Tolerance is not God's Agape Love. Acceptance is not God's Agape Love. Inclusion is not God's Agape Love unless it is inclusion in His ark of safety. Inclusion at the foot of *The* Cross and real transformation and change of heart first and then behaviors. Cain thought it was okay to approach the Living God anyway Cain saw fit but that was wrong. Parts of religious circles and ecumenicalism are portraying the "faith" as if it is okay to ignore the LORD's holy standards in favor of *majority rule* and committee votes in the *hellish affirmative.* Is it the anti-gospel according to Cain? Is it a synthetic gospel?

The message of *The* Cross is that the Living God loves us too much to leave us the way we were born. That is why Jesus told the top teaching religious leader of His earthly day, "...you must be born again!" Hey Lady, we were all born the wrong way – dead in trespasses and sin according to Ephesians 2:1. So, if you were born in a way which is contrary to the way of the Living God; then *The* Cross offers you the opportunity to be born again. 2nd Corinthians 5:19 and Colossians 2:13 tell us that the rebirth begins with the sin and trespasses being forgiven. Then the new living begins.

Just as the Supreme Doctor of Creation told Israel's top religious teacher that he needed to be born again; He is offering you the same diagnosis of your spiritual condition and prognosis if you reject His remedy. Being born again is also being born from above by the Spirit of the Living God.

It is important to note that the sanctification process includes keeping established commandments as well as practicing repentance. Being anxious to repent is very important in the sanctification process. The invitation to come boldly to the throne of grace is by implication a mandate to repent when needed; to stay in the fellowship. What fellowship? Maybe the one with the Father and the Son. (Isaiah 2:5; 1 John 1:7)

9 Know you not that the unrighteous[not right with God] shall not inherit the kingdom of God? Be not deceived: neither fornicators, nor idolaters, nor adulterers, nor effeminate, nor abusers of themselves with mankind,
10 Nor thieves, nor covetous, nor drunkards, nor revilers, nor extortionist, shall inherit the kingdom of God. 1 Corinthians 6:9-10

Fairness is at the heart of what the Living God does. He loves us too much not to tell us the truth. God loves us too much not to tell us what is bad for us. He loves us too much not to warn us of consequences. God loves us too much to leave us the way we were. He loves me too much to leave me the way I was. He loves you too much to leave you the way you are. Anyone teaching that we can do it contrary to the way which the Living God has laid out is lying to you.

Anyone believing that they can be right with the Living God in ways other than those prescribed by the Living God is lying to himself or herself. The kingdom of the Living God is not a democracy. Committee consensus cannot override the mandates of the Living God. Denominational leadership endorsing what the Living God says is wrong cannot make it right. Doesn't the blood cover it? No. No. No.

Anyone teaching that the blood of Jesus' cross covers the deliberate violation of God's standards is lying to you. Anyone accepting such teaching is lying to themselves. Anyone teaching that because Jesus shed His blood for sins that He established a license to sin is lying to you. Anyone accepting such teaching is lying to themselves. Teachers at supposed Bible Schools and churches teaching that sexual and immoral activity which the Living God says is against His standards is okay because *The* Cross forgives it all are false teachers and lying messengers of darkness. (2nd Corinthians 11:13-15, 2nd Peter 2:9-15, Jude 1:10-15) Don't fall for the lies. Desire the truth. Value the truth.

Truth is extremely important to eternal security. The word of the Living God says that those who value their desires and agendas more than the truth will qualify to be deceived by the devil and his cohorts such as the antichrist and false prophet. That group will do what looks like good works and wonderful deeds but they will be founded on lies and introduced by the spirit of death.

8 And then shall that Wicked be revealed, whom the Lord shall consume with the spirit of his mouth, and shall destroy with the brightness of his coming:

*9 Even him, whose coming is after the working of Satan with all power and signs and **lying wonders**,*

*10 And with all deceivableness of unrighteousness in **them that perish; because they received not the love of the truth**, that they might be saved.*

11 And for this cause God shall send them strong delusion, that they should believe a lie:

12 That they all might be damned who believed not the truth, but had pleasure in unrighteousness.

2 Thessalonians 2:8-12

One example of strong delusion is believing you can engage in wrong behavior and deliberately violate the standards of the Living God and not repent of it. Forgiveness is a critical part of the sanctification process as is repentance. John said in his first letter to the church at large, "If you do sin, Jesus is your advocate [legal defense] with the Father." If you did not need to ask repentance; then you would not need a defender.   If we did not need to

THE CROSS MADE *ALL* THE DIFFERENCE

repent then the accuser would be unemployed. The fact that Jesus is defending the new creation believer IF they sin is proof positive that anyone telling you that you do not have to repent is lying to you.

Even good works can be evil when tainted by depraved motivations. Jesus urged the religious leaders to make the inner life the priority and not superficial pretense. Religion seeks for solutions to humanity's brokenness in behavioral modification. Psychoanalysis seeks for solutions to humanity's brokenness in the brain/mind. That is not deep enough. Secular humanism and fake science (1st Timothy 6:20) accept the flaws and simply blames a blind designer for the brokenness.

Highly educated fools have said in their hearts that there is no God (Psalm 14:1/53:1) and use every bit of their broken essence to prove it. In the absence of proof they resort to scientific and social propaganda. On the other hand, mind study and behavioral modification don't dig deep enough to deal with the real problem. The natural or dead spirit core is the problem. Studying the mind won't fix the broken spirit core but a resurrected spirit core can repair the mind and body.

Revamping behavior to alter or control the

fallen flesh won't fix the broken spirit core but a resurrected spirit core will cause the fallen flesh to lose its power to dominate behavior. The real problem is one that only God can fix. The spirit and soul are both mysterious to us and we talk of them interchangeably but God knows the difference between the two. His scalpel is so precise that it can cut along the dividing line between the spirit and the soul.

12 For the word of God is quick, and powerful, and sharper than any two-edged sword, piercing even to the [separation between]soul and spirit, and of the joints and marrow, and is a discerner of the thoughts and intents of the heart.
13 Neither is there any creature that is not manifest in his sight: but all things are naked and opened unto the eyes of him with whom we have to do. Hebrews 4:12-13

How could anyone think that the *Supreme Designer* is blind when God can do work which is infinitely more intricate that any we can imagine? We read of it in these few verses and still cannot imagine what is involved. Not only can the Living God separate the dead spirit core from the rest of the human construct but He can also delineate between thoughts, feelings, emotions, and motivations of the heart. It makes more sense to be in the hands of the Living God than those of an evolving theory.

So, the Word of the Living God obviously plays an important part in the sanctification process in light of Hebrews 4:12. Just as Jesus told the religious leaders that the Kingdom of God was in them [via Word of God and Hebrew alephbet?]; that Word filled Holy Spirit would reside in the new creation believers and discern the intents, motivation, and thoughts and guide the believer in the proper paths. Because humanity is part of the equation, things won't always go exactly the way they should but God is patient and has many options at His disposal.

Listen to Jesus' promise of the eventual indwelling of the Living God in the new creation believers:

16 And I will pray the Father, and he shall give you another Comforter, that he may abide with you forever;
*17 Even **the Spirit of truth**; whom the world cannot receive, because it sees him not, neither knows him: but you know him; for he [journeys] with you, and **shall be in you**.*   John 14:16-17

See that? The *Spirit of Truth* not only would

dwell within but He is along for the ride in the Christian journey. The Holy Spirit is not in some dormant state inside the believer waiting for the *sweet by and by* to begin but He is actively involved in what I would call "coaching" us in this Christian walk which Romans 6:4 calls the new life –new man- in contrast to the old death –the old man. The Spirit of the Living God hid from the old man behind a thick curtain under the old covenant simply to protect the individual from dying from the cataclysmic contact of the sin nature with God's holy nature.

But now, because of the blood of *The* Cross, He has given us part in His divine nature. As I type that sentence I pray that I am not being irreverent; but grace has to be more amazing than how we've taught and learned it over the years. We say grace is amazing then respond in the most ungracious ways when people sin, fall, make mistakes, or backslide.

Here is some evidence, I hope, to the affirmative that grace is more amazing than we've thought or taught:

2 Grace and peace be multiplied to you in [the] knowledge of God and of Jesus our Lord.
*3 As **his divine power has given to us all things** which relate to life and godliness, through the*

knowledge of him that has called us by glory and virtue,

*4 through which he has given to us the greatest and precious promises, that through these **you may become partakers** of [the] divine nature, having escaped the corruption that is in the world through lust.*   2 Peter 1:2-4 Darby

*And what agreement has the temple of God with idols? For **you are the temple** of the living God. As God has said: "**I will dwell in them** And walk among them. I will be their God, And they shall be My people."*   2 Corinthians 6:16

Under the Old Covenant, the Living God kept His *Kingdom Spirit* behind that thick curtain in the temple to protect the people from the glory. On the day Jesus was crucified, that veil was torn from top to bottom because *The* Cross opened the door for the individual indwelling. That's right, the Spirit of God broke out of the veil to take up residence in us.

Some teachers make a point out of us going behind the veil but He is not behind the veil anymore. He vacated the Holy of Holies on Resurrection Day, chomping at the bit, preparing to relocate to the new Holy of Holies INSIDE the new creation believers.

*17 Therefore, **if** anyone is in Christ, he is **a new creation**; the old has gone, the new has come!*
*18 All this is from God, who **reconciled us to himself** through Christ and gave us the ministry of reconciliation:*
19 that God was reconciling the world to himself in Christ, not counting men's sins against them. And he has committed to us the message of reconciliation. 2 Corinthians 5:17-19 NIV

The Spirit of the Living God is now inside us using the Word to coach us through this new life and all the while imparting the imputed perfection of Jesus **in us on a permanent basis**. He is the express presence of God inhabiting the new creation believer and teaching us the *exceeding great and precious promises* (2nd Peter 1:4) which include partaking of the divine nature of the Living God being **imparted to us on a continually permanent basis**. That is the mercy we obtain at the throne of grace where we find more necessary grace for each new challenge. As amazing as grace is unfolding to be in this journey; the Living God has so much that He gives more and more grace if we need it.(James 4:6)

4 You adulterers and adulteresses, know you not

that the friendship of the world is enmity with God? whosoever therefore will be a friend of the world is the enemy of God.

5 Do you think that the scripture says in vain, The spirit that dwells in us lusts to envy?

*6 But **he gives more grace**. Wherefore he says, God resists the proud, but gives grace **unto the humble**.*

7 Submit yourselves therefore to God. Resist the devil, and he will flee from you.

*8 Draw nigh to God, and he will draw nigh to you. Cleanse your hands, you sinners; and **purify your hearts**, you double minded.* James 4:4-8

The Spirit of the Living God is inside the new creation believers coaching them towards an awesome destination according to 2nd Corinthians 3:18 but along the way and especially early on following the enticements of the old nature will be a challenge.

*But **we all**, with open face beholding as in a glass the glory of the Lord, **are changed into the same image from glory to glory**, even as by the Spirit of the Lord.* 2 Corinthians 3:18

It is easy for us to be triggered by our former puppeteer -the sin nature- and engage in the bondage we were delivered from. That old behavior is comfortable and familiar and easily entreated. However, if we need more strength to endure; then there is more grace made available as long as we are willing to humble ourselves. When we succumb to the pull of that old nature – the devil – and reengage in behavior we were disengaged from by *The* Cross of Christ; the Word says to simply humble ourselves to God and He will give us the added grace we need to push back against the pull of the old nature. And the result?

Submit *yourselves therefore to God.* **Resist** *the devil [old nature],* **and he will flee from you**.

James 4:7

Humbling ourselves [repenting and asking forgiveness] to the sanctifying influence of Holy Spirit results in grace to resist the old nature and it fleeing from us. That means that the Living God's Spirit is aiding us from the inside out as well as the outside in. With Him being in us that also means that all that He is resides in us as well. He is the kingdom according to Romans 14:17 and brings the kingdom with Him when He takes of residence in the new creation believer. When Jesus told His disciples of the promised indwelling of the Holy Spirit; He finished the statement in John 14:18 with, "I will come to you." Jesus, in the person of the Holy Spirit, has inhabited the new creation believers. So, that means that all that is in Jesus is in us as well. How can this be?

9 For in [Christ] dwells all the fullness of the Godhead bodily.
10 And you are complete in him, which is the head of all principality and power: Colossians 2:9-10

Hear what Charles Haddon Spurgeon's revelation of Colossians 2:9-10 spells out and celebrates:

All the attributes of Christ, as God and man, are at our disposal. All the fullness of the Godhead, whatever that marvelous term may comprehend, is ours to make us complete. He cannot endow us with the attributes of Deity; but He has done all that can be done, **for He has made even His divine power and Godhead subservient to our salvation**. His omnipotence, omniscience, omnipresence, immutability and infallibility, are all combined for our defense. Arise, believer, and behold the Lord Jesus yoking the whole of His divine Godhead to the chariot of salvation! How vast His grace, how firm His faithfulness, how unswerving His immutability, how infinite His power, how limitless His knowledge!

All these are by the Lord Jesus made the pillars of the temple of salvation; and all, without diminution of their infinity, are covenanted [contract-blood oath] to us as our perpetual inheritance. The fathomless love of the Savior's heart is every drop of it ours; every sinew in the arm of might, every jewel in the crown of majesty, the immensity of divine knowledge, and the sternness of divine justice, all are ours, and shall be employed for us.

The whole of Christ, in His adorable character as the Son of God, is by Himself made over to us most richly to enjoy. His wisdom is our direction, His knowledge our instruction, His power our protection, His justice our surety, His love our comfort, His mercy our solace, and His immutability our trust. He makes no reserve, but opens the recesses of the Mount of God and bids us dig in its mines for the hidden treasures.

"All, all, all are yours," says He, "be you satisfied with favor and full of the goodness of the Lord."

Oh! how sweet thus to behold Jesus, and to call upon Him with the certain confidence that in seeking the interposition of His love or power, we are but asking for that which He has already faithfully promised. [and given – my words] **(From Spurgeon's *Morning and Evening* Devotional; Excerpt from AM Devotion for May 18.)**

If all of these assertions and revelations are accurate then that means that the entire divinity team of Heaven is at work in us helping us to become what *The* Cross of Christ has already made us...just like Jesus. Whoa!

But we Christians have no veil over our faces; we can be mirrors that brightly reflect the glory of the Lord. And as the Spirit of the Lord works within us, we become more and more like him.

2 Corinthians 3:18 TLB

This verse is exciting in all versions so I suggest you read as many as you can. The bottom line is the Spirit of the Living God has turned the light back on in the spirit core of new creation believers. That light was snuffed out by the sin nature when Adam gave it all away. *The* Cross opened the door to our spirit core and the light of the Living God got back in there and...BANG! He says inside every new creation believer, "LIGHT BE!" The light of the Spirit of the Living Father explodes inside the dead spirit core and His light is good. Very good. Amazing grace!

The church has done a poor job of teaching sanctification over the years for a number of reasons. **First**, we weren't really sure how to teach it because the leadership was having the same flesh challenges as everyone else and couldn't reconcile the behavior, motivations, and thought-life we knew we were supposed to engage in and that which we actually had. That in mind, we didn't want showing empathy and understanding resulting in an impression of a license to sin. We forgot that a license wasn't needed. The sin nature and its Pavlovian triggers were already in full effect.

Second, we didn't understand grace then the way we are beginning to now. The prophet Daniel predicted that the closer we got to the end of the age that, "knowledge would be on the increase." That knowledge is not just technology, science, and the realization that evolution will never graduate from a theory to a law. Theology, the study of the Living God, will also increase in knowledge. Just as Martin Luther understood more about grace and faith than the believers fifty years earlier did, theologians and believers who came fifty years afterwards had a better grasp than Luther did.

We would not have thought fifty years ago to teach a new convert that after their *come-to-Jesus moment* that the first thing that MIGHT happen to them is wanting to get back to the bar or brothel. We needed to teach that once a person is in Christ and immediately becomes a new creation that **the old habits and behaviors don't disappear** like magic for most. If we had taught that critical point; then we would not have had so many converts leave the church in many cases never to return because they thought that the grace thing did not work and *The* Cross thing didn't take. LORD have mercy!

We know more now than we did then and will disciple correctly and not throw people away because they exhibit their ugly humanity after coming to Christ. If we understood then what we do now, then the church people with the Pharisee spirit wouldn't be projecting their own struggles and failures on those around them and chasing real converts away. The Lord winked at certain ignorance in the past (Acts 17:30) but now demands a change of mindset – repentance. If we understand grace accurately then we would be sure to extend the same revelation of grace to others which God's mirror has shown us of ourselves. Imagine if all of the brief converts which we lost or ran away from the church were discipled with the teaching of the Almighty's grace mirror?

Now, back to the behaviors which result in denied admission into the Kingdom of the Living God. Verses nine and ten of the sixth chapter of 1st Corinthians list behaviors which hearken back to what we were before *The* Cross. This portion scripture is crystal clear that those who engage in such behavior will not inherit the kingdom.

What we understand about ourselves and the transition between what we used to be and what we are going to be makes the verses which follow extremely exciting. Following the list of disqualifying behaviors we read in 1st Corinthians 6:11:

*And such WERE some of you: but you are **washed**, but you are **sanctified**, but you are **justified** in the name of the Lord Jesus, and by the Spirit of our God.*

Such abhorrent behavior is simply washed away by *The* Cross? What's more is the exciting news which comes later in the sixth chapter of

1st Corinthians.

19 What? know you not that **your body is the temple of the Holy Ghost** *which is in you, which you have of God, and you are not your own?*
20 For you are bought with a price: therefore glorify God in **your body**, **and** *in* **your spirit**, *which* **are God's**.　　　1 Corinthians 6:19-20

If my experiences and those of people I've spoken and prayed with are typical then those disqualifying behaviors don't just go away like someone waved a wand and poof...no more evil tendencies. On the contrary, those behaviors fight to remain. They call you in the middle of the night and greet you in the cool of the day. They seem as close as they've ever been. Still, the Word of the Living God says that the new creation believer has been:

Washed!　　　**Sanctified!**　　　**Justified!**

If you read that entire chapter you will find the discussion is about grace. The grace of the Living God is quite amazing so don't blow it by behaving the way you used to. Repent quickly and get back on course. That is the genesis of the question Paul poses, "Don't you know that God dwells within you?" That is supposed to change the way we think, believe, and behave. That's sanctification. Our outside paradigm shifts as we understand the new inside paradigm reality *The Cross of Jesus* established.

Let me be clear. The subject of sanctification has not been taught properly, accurately, and in many churches at all because it is difficult to comprehend with the natural mind. We know how we are to behave and think following our come-to-Jesus moment; but how we actually behave and think are diametrically opposed to how we should. We live and feel like we are still sinners but we know that we are not but can't reconcile it. If we attempt to teach sanctification straight from the Bible; some will be accused of offering a license to sin.

On the contrary, the proper teaching of sanctification gives hope of real freedom from the slavery of sin. Biblical sanctification is liberating. Religious sanctification is simply trading the puppeteer of the old man for a new puppeteer. Religious carrots and sticks which at times we use to beat ourselves. Guilty Catholics employ the Holy Spirit but struggle with the works of penance. Baptists have hoped to free themselves from the old man via baptismal waters. The waters help only if you understand that it re-enacts the resurrection of your dead human spirit.

Pentecostals have condemned to Hell those who do not speak in tongues by misusing Romans 8:9. Wearing doilies on your head and long skirts don't make you sanctified and holy. You can be sanctified looking on the outside and filthy on the inside. Dead even. Don't get me wrong. Modesty is part of the adorning of the spirit which the Word speaks of in the third chapter of 1st Peter. Inner sanctification is a higher priority than superficial show.

Woe unto you, scribes and Pharisees, hypocrites! for you are like [white washed tombs], which indeed appear beautiful outward, but are within full of dead men's bones, and of all uncleanness.
                                                    Matthew 23:27

The publican of Luke 18 went to his home justified compared to the esteemed Pharisee which dotted and crossed all of the religious i's and t's and even reminded God of it in his public prayer. The Pharisee should have done what he claimed he was doing but made the mistake of comparing himself to a standard other than God's. He compared himself to a shunned member of society rather than to the only standard that matters – God's word. God's standards of approaching Him.

The esteemed religious leader, Jesus said, wasn't justified. Obviously, self justification doesn't do us any good with God. The publican, though, wouldn't even look up towards the representation of God – the scrolls – but simply beat on his chest (symbolic of the location of the sinfulness) and pled for mercy. On the outside, these two looked obviously righteous and unrighteous. On the inside, the opposite was true.

Wouldn't it be better to be filthy on the outside but sanctified on the inside? Remember the context before you judge that statement. Eventually, the inside comes out and dominates the outside.   Yes, modesty is a virtue taught in the holy scriptures but it goes on to speak of dressing the spirit. The only way to properly dress the spirit is with the Word. Proper teaching, preaching, and understanding of the word of the Living God will dress your spirit core *to the nines.* (idiom meaning perfection)

I hope I am being clear. Sanctification is twofold. You can tell from these scriptures utilized so far that the main part of sanctification is what the Living God does for us, in us, *and to us* to make us something His Spirit can reside in.

The other part of sanctification is our cooperation with the Holy Spirit. We must yield to His coaching and guidance. It is clear from scripture that when the Living God sanctifies the new believer He immediately, at the core, makes them what they are going to be. Our cooperating with the Holy Spirit living in the new temple is the sanctification which starts the process of our outside catching up with our inside or the new inside coming to the surface to manifest the sons of the Living God.

All of creation waits with eager longing for God to reveal his sons.   Romans 8:19 TEV

But we Christians have no veil over our faces; we can be mirrors that brightly reflect the glory of the Lord. And as the Spirit of the Lord works within us, we become more and more like him.
                    2 Corinthians 3:18 TLB

When you learn that the mirror of God's word shows you what you really are on the inside; you should develop a desire to look into His mirror to know Him and to find yourself. Kenneth Hagin has been quoted as saying that when people are brainwashed by religion they stop paying attention to their Bibles. I suggest to you that the Living God wants us hungry for His word because it will lead to more of Him and a better understanding of ourselves as new creation believers. We will find in the Word information about our new identity as well as understand our old identity better.

And I am sure that God who began the good work within you will keep right on helping you grow in his grace until his task within you is finally finished on that day when Jesus Christ returns.

Philippians 1:6 TLB

As we search the Word of the Living God, we will get the revelation that the same *good work* which He is performing in us is what He is performing in our brother and sister (as well as yet to be brothers and sisters); and will cause us to extend grace like never before. If the Pharisee of Luke chapter 18 understood grace, then he would have been gracious to the publican and realized that it was God's grace which allowed him to be the person he was. Instead, he looked into the wrong mirror – self righteousness and self justification. We are suppose to give the same grace we receive. That is why we restore the fallen in a spirit of meekness and not kick them while they are down or kill the wounded like a beta attempting to take over the pride from the alpha.

*6 Brethren, if a man be overtaken in a fault, **you which are spiritual**, restore such a one in the spirit of meekness; considering thyself, lest thou also be tempted.*
2 Bear you one another's burdens, and so fulfill the law of Christ. [humility and agape love?]
3 For if a man think himself to be something, when he is nothing, he deceives himself.
4 But let every man prove his own work, and then shall he have rejoicing in himself alone, and not in another. Galatians 6:1-4

Here is a litmus test directly from Heaven. If we are not restoring the fallen then obviously we are not walking in agape love. We may be walking in indifference. If we are attempting to restore the fallen using condemnation and guilt then we are probably using a foundation of religion. IF we are restoring the fallen in humility, love, and a spirit of meekness; then and only then are we spiritual.

When it comes to falling, that "IF" shows up again. Paul doesn't say, "when a brother falls," but, "if a brother falls," once again giving credence to the fact that the new creation believer is no longer a slave to its former puppeteer –the sin nature. The mirror of God's word gives us gauges to measure our spirituality and maturity in many cases. In this case, we can measure our spirituality by how we treat and respond to the fallen brother or sister. All because of the new resident inside our spirit core. All that He is came with Him. Even the ability to teach us from the inside out.

*27 But **the anointing** which you have received of him **abides within you**, and you need not that any man teach you: but as **the same anointing** teaches you of all things, and **is truth, and is** no lie, and even as it has taught you, you shall abide in **him**.*
28 And now, little children, abide in him; that, when he shall appear, we may have confidence, and not be ashamed before him at his coming.
*29 If you know that he is righteous, you know that every one that does **[produces]** righteousness is born of him.* 1 John 2:27-29

For the phrase "*does righteousness*" in verse twenty-nine above, the Greek word translated, *does* means to create or produce. The anointing which the Old Covenant believers experienced was topical and temporary. There are many accounts of the Spirit coming upon chosen and cooperative ones but for a short period of time. First Peter 1:23 says that the incorruptible seed of the Word dwells in us forever. The new creation believer has an anointing that won't go away. An anointing which gives the new creation believer the capacity to produce righteousness. An anointing which is not temporary but has taken up permanent residence in our resurrected spirit core. How can that be?

Jesus told us it would happen but it took awhile for us to connect the dots. Even where *The* Cross of Christ has been preached we have evaded painting the complete picture because it feels and sounds so sacrilegious and even profane to the religious mind. If you survey the book of Leviticus for the word profane you may come to the conclusion that what the Word calls profane is to speak of and treat as common that which is far from common to the Living God. I am simply going to list the scriptures which paint the complete picture of what *The* Cross has done in us.

16 And I will pray the Father, and he shall give you another Comforter, that he may abide with you forever;
*17 Even **the Spirit of truth**; whom the world*

cannot receive, because it sees him not, neither knows him: but you know him; for he dwells with you, and **shall be in you**.

18 I will not leave you comfortless: **I will come to you**.   John 14:16-18

16 A little while, and you shall not see me: and again, a little while, **and you shall see me, because I go to the Father.**

19 Now Jesus knew that they were desirous to ask him, and said unto them, Do you inquire among yourselves of that I said, A little while, and you shall not see me: and again, a little while, and you shall see me?

20 Verily, verily, I say unto you, That you shall weep and lament, but the world shall rejoice: and you shall be sorrowful, but your sorrow shall be turned into joy.   John 16:16, 19-20

But when **the Comforter is** *come, whom I will send unto you from the Father, even* **the Spirit of truth**, *which proceeds from the Father, he shall testify of me:*   John 15:26

22 And the glory which you gave me I have given them; that they may be one, even as we are one:

23 **I in them**, *and* **you in me**, *that they may be made perfect in one; and that the world may know* *that **you** have sent me, and **have loved them, as thou have loved me.***   John 17:22-23

25 O righteous Father, the world has not known thee: but I have known thee, and these have known that thou hast sent me.

*26 And I have declared unto them thy name, and will declare it: that the love wherewith thou hast loved me may be in them, **AND I IN THEM.***

      John 17:25-26

*45 And so it is written, The first man Adam was made a living soul; the last Adam was made a quickening **[life giving] spirit**.*

46 Howbeit that was not first which is spiritual, but that which is natural; and afterward that which is spiritual.

47 The first man is of the earth, earthy: the second man is the Lord from heaven.   1st Cor. 15:45-47

*17 Now **the Lord is that Spirit**: and where the Spirit of the Lord is, there is liberty.*

18 But we all, with open face beholding as in a glass the glory of the Lord, are changed into the same image from glory to glory, even as by the Spirit of the Lord.   2 Corinthians 3:17-18

Do you see what I see? *The* Cross has made

us extremely uncommon. It is an absolute insult to the redemptive work of Jesus, the sanctifying ministry of the "Holy Spirit," and the transformative impact of Jesus' cross to call yourself a sinner saved by grace. There is no such thing in the scriptures. When we fall for that **religious tripe**; we profane what the Living God and Father of our Lord Jesus Christ has done because of, for, and in us through *The* Cross. This covenant of grace is exceedingly abundantly above amazing.

Think about **what you know of yourself**. The darkness. The trash in your heart. The past and present imperfect. Now, think about **what the Word says about you**. I know. Those two pictures don't agree with each other. That is why it is important to gaze into the glory of the Living God's Word to see what His mirror is showing you of yourself. It shows what you really are on the inside. You can agree with the mirror of your past memories and shame or you can agree with His Word. You can agree with the mirror of religious condemnation or you can agree with His Word. You can agree with the promises and prayers Yeshua/Jesus prayed for you in the fourteenth to seventeenth chapters of John's gospel or you can profane the picture of you which the Word of the Living God paints.

Can you honestly review the few scriptures presented in this and the previous chapter and relegate yourself to something which is not mentioned in the Word at all? **Once you are saved by grace; the Word of God no longer calls you a sinner**. The only title the Living God gives you after salvation is saint. From dead in trespasses and sins (Ephesians 2:1) to a saint (1st Corinthians 1:2) simply by putting faith in *The* Cross? That is so much more than amazing.

Grace upon grace!

CHAPTER FOUR

I KNOW IT WAS
THE BLOOD
THAT SAVED ME

*He has delivered us from the power of darkness and conveyed us into the kingdom of the Son of His love, in whom we have **redemption through His blood**, the forgiveness of sins.*

Colossians 1:13-14

The *African American Heritage Hymnal* is one of a few hymnals which have one of the most sung blood memorial hymns of the Baptist church. *I Know It Was The Blood* is sung nearly every Communion Sunday and any spring or fall revival. Some of the most popular songs heard in Black Baptist churches are songs which one may be hard pressed to find in print. *Oh The Blood*

Done Sign My Name is another popular song heard during the aforementioned events. The redeeming power of Yeshua Jesus' atoning blood has been memorialized for eons and celebrated in song for centuries. Obviously, the blood harkens back to *The* Cross of Christ. Even festive Christmas carols and stage celebrations make it crystal clear that there is no Christmas without *The* Cross. *"Peace on earth and goodwill towards men"* IS a proclamation of grace. The war can be ended if we accept the Almighty's peace treaty-*The* Cross.

The writer of the letter to the Hebrews laid a strong foundation of righteousness through the understanding of the blood of Yeshua Jesus. The fourth chapter ends with the invitation for all to come boldly to the throne of grace based on Jesus' performance and not our own. The tenth chapter tells us that Jesus' blood will eternally perfect the sanctified ones. The ones who put faith in that blood.

His blood is so powerful that it speaks blessings over us in life and advocates for us in the arena of accusation. (Zechariah 3:1/Revelation 12:10) Listen to what the twelfth chapter of Hebrews says about Jesus' blood:

*To the general assembly and church of the firstborn, which are written in heaven, and to God the Judge of all, and to the spirits of just men made perfect, And to Jesus the mediator of the **new covenant, and to the blood** of sprinkling, **that speaks better things than that of Abel.***

Hebrews 12:23-24

You can find the account of Abel's murder- in the fourth chapter of Genesis if you require a detailed synopsis. Now, I honestly intended this to be a brief work. In a politically correct social environment in which the length of Sunday worship services are in danger of being reduced to some type of ecclesiastical drive thru or microwaved message; one tends to take into consideration the short attention span we have to Biblical, religious, and spiritual things. Sadly, though, not all spiritual things get the least of our attention. The spiritual things which the Living God has warned us not to delve into get our attention unabashedly. Psychics, tarot ciphers, and other dark spirit mediums have to tell their disciples, "Time's up," while the congregations of the church plead for shorter services. The humanity!

In light of what Jesus' cross does for, in, and through us, it is no stretch to conclude that it was that blood that *never loses its power* that made it all possible.   Just as the blood sprinkled on the mercy seat in the Holy of Holies reminded the avenging angels of the mercy of the Living God; the blood of Yeshua Jesus speaks mercy, grace, and protection.

After Abel's murder, God gave Cain a chance to confess and plead for mercy but he wouldn't say the right thing. All Cain would do was lie. Even after he was judged, he wouldn't admit what he did. The Living God informed Cain that Abel's blood cried out from the ground. Although we are not told exactly what Abel's blood said, we have a good idea based on Hebrews 12:24.

We know what Jesus' blood speaks based on His words while He was being crucified. "Forgive them Father because they don't realize what they are doing," is an astounding statement when you consider the suffering. It is also astounding to think that the one being executed was praying for His Roman and Jewish executioners.

For Abel's blood to speak inferior things compared to what the blood of Jesus speaks means one can conclude that Abel wasn't praying for Cain as his life was pouring out. Abel was not asking for forgiveness for his killer.

*24 You have come to Jesus, the one who mediates
the new covenant between God and people, and to
the sprinkled blood, which speaks of forgiveness
instead of crying out for vengeance like the
blood of Abel.*
*25 Be careful that you do not refuse to listen to the
One who is speaking. For if the people of Israel did
not escape when they refused to listen to Moses,
the earthly messenger, we will certainly not
escape if we reject the One who speaks to us from
heaven!* Hebrews 12:24-25 NLT

We can be sure that Abel's blood spoke
because the Living God told Cain that He heard
its voice. Amazingly, the Living God and Creator
not only understands the language of tears but
He also speaks blood. Thank God He does
because Jesus' blood has something to say to us
and on behalf of us as our advocate. So, is it
possible that Abel's last thoughts, emotions, and
especially words gave specific voice to his blood?
Now, if Cain had confessed and sought
forgiveness; he could have experienced a
different outcome rather than be "marked" as a
murderer. Regardless of Abel's plea for
vengeance, Cain could have found forgiveness.

Just before the murder, the Living God talks
with Cain of a sin purifying sacrifice just waiting

for him "at the door." He appeared to have trouble sacrificing an animal but no misgivings about killing his own brother. Now, as Abel's life was pouring out of him following Cain's attack; Abel's response to what was happening to him left an impression on his blood. The Almighty even told Cain that the blood of Abel was speaking to HIM from the grave. Blood is so much more significant than we have come to understand. Yes, if it stays inside your body then you have a higher chance of staying alive but blood has a voice based on what the closing emotions and words of the one passing from this world into eternity exhibits. Let's hear these two voices of blood:

Abel's Blood   Jesus' Blood

Abel's Blood	Jesus' Blood
Revenge	**Forgiveness**
Vengeance	**Mercy**
Justice	**Justification**
(his rights)	(others' rights)

At the moment of death, I'm surmising, blood can curse or it can bless. That must mean that Abel had the option of blessing instead of cursing. Some Bible teachers have called Abel a type of Christ but in this case Abel doesn't qualify. Why? Abel's blood spoke vengeance while Jesus, as He was dying, prayed for God to forgive his executioners. Their last words and emotions were imprinted on their blood.

Years ago, I was invited to a funeral of someone I had never met so I have no context for what I'm about to say. The person in the casket had an expression on the face, which I have never seen before on a corpse. I have seen it before on the living and it looked allot like anger. On the surface, it looked like this individual died angry.(my opinion)   Again, I have no context because the funeral was the first time I encountered this "individual." Obviously, the individual was gone and only the shell –the earth suit- was in the casket.   The person's last emotions and words stamped an expression on the face at the point of death. I hope I am wrong about that funeral experience. How unfortunate to enter eternity angry rather than at peace or regretful rather than happy. *The* Cross can help with both of those endings. Lord, have mercy!

Yeshua stamped His blood with grace and mercy from the beginning. When He returns to His home town after His post-baptism wilderness testing; Yeshua/Jesus preached with such grace and never-seen-before authority that

He was dragged to a cliff to be thrown off. We know He sweated drops of blood in Gethsemane but is it possible the same happened in the wilderness for forty days laying the foundation of His redemption ministry? That's right. His wasn't simply a healing ministry although He healed all types of sicknesses' and diseases.

Jesus' was not simply a speaking ministry although His words saved souls, shut down storms, and drove out devils. His wasn't simply a miracle ministry although He gave sight to the blind-born, gave "walk" to the crippled-born, gave hearing to the deaf, and even raised two people from the dead.

Jesus' ministry [full of grace and truth -John 1:14] was first and foremost a redemption ministry. His was a search and rescue mission ministry. The healings and miracles were His advertising to draw as many as possible to hear *the good news of the kingdom*. Search for the lost and rescue them from God's judgment. His entire mission was about grace, forgiveness, mercy, and the truth about what the Living God is really like and how He feels about us.

But even the very hairs of your head are all numbered. Fear not therefore: you are of more value than many sparrows.   Luke 12:7

Fear not, little flock; for it is your Father's good pleasure to give you the kingdom.   Luke 12:32

33 And when they were come to the place, which is called Calvary, there they crucified him, and the malefactors, one on the right hand, and the other on the left.
34 Then said Jesus, Father, forgive them; for they know not what they do.   Luke 23:33-34

In contrast to Abel's "*last will and testament*" which cried out for revenge, Jesus' blood established a new covenant called grace. Take a look:

10 But this is the new covenant I will make with the people of Israel on that day, says the Lord: I will put my laws in their minds, and I will write them on their hearts. I will be their God, and they will be my people.
11 And they will not need to teach their neighbors, nor will they need to teach their relatives, saying, 'You should know the Lord.' For everyone, from the least to the greatest, will know me already.

*12 And **I will forgive their wickedness**, and **I will never again remember their sins**."*
Hebrews 8:10-12

"I will not remember their sins ever again? But how? Why? For the new creation believer, sins were already judged and punished in Yeshua Jesus on *The* Cross. Does that make *The* Cross the *sea of forgetfulness*? In Micah 7:19, the prophet predicts that the Most High God will "have compassion on us and throw our sins in the depths of the sea." Once something sinks in a large body of water and the swirl dissipates, there is no evidence that the sunken object ever existed. Psalm 103:12 tells us that our Heavenly Scapegoat has separated us from our sins forever. I know Micah doesn't say, "*sea of forgetfulness,*" but the implication is clear. Also, the word "remember" is not only referring to the opposite of forgetting but also the opposite of "dismember." Dismember means to dismantle or tear apart while remember means to put back together.

The Living God promises to no longer associate those confessed, forgiven, and tossed away sins with us ever again. (Psalm 103:12/Hebrews 8:12) He promises to no longer associate them with me again. He promises to no longer associate your repented sins with you ever again. Do you see how much more better things the blood of Jesus spoke compared to the blood of Abel? If I was in church right now, I would probably scream, "Glory!" Never mind that. I just did.

Because of the blood of Yeshua Jesus, we can be sure that the Living God will not associate our sins with us any longer and because our redemption covered the past, present, and future;[iv] we can repent of sins in our body, thought life, emotions, and anger and trust that they will be added to Micah's sea of forgetfulness never to be retrieved – except by us. Yes, we make the mistake of asking for forgiveness of the same thing over and over and sometimes for years and years depending on how egregious it was.

Can you imagine the members of the Godhead looking at each other shrugging their shoulders [poetic imagination] when they hear a prayer of forgiveness for something that was already dealt with years ago? What about days or even minutes ago? The Living God [who cannot lie - Titus 1:2] has promised to forget repented and forgiven sins so when we bring them up again after repenting; I imagine Heaven saying, "What is she talking about?" "What is he talking about?"

Let us therefore come boldly unto the throne of grace, that we may obtain mercy, and find grace to help in time of need.   Hebrews 4:16

Hebrews tells us to come boldly to the throne of grace for good reason! The blood of Jesus has paved the way, washed us clean, and opened up the Holy of Holies to each and every one of us as was the original intent. The Living God invited all of the up to six million former Egyptian slaves to have the same relationship with Him as Moses had. We are the peculiar royal priesthood (1st Peter 2:9) because of *The* Cross. They all could have Jesus put things right with His blood. He put us right with His blood. He put me right with His blood. He put you right with His blood. Yes, even me. Yes, even you. Take it!

We all have those voices telling us things that are contrary to what the word of the Living God says about us. (Romans 3:4) We have to remember to, *"let the [Word of the Living God] be true and every other voice a liar."* So, when the voices of religious slavery and condemnation tell you that you need to "do something" that makes you feel right with God again you should tell that voice, "The blood speaks better things!"

When that religious condemnation voice tells you that you need to do enough good to outweigh those bad things you did, you need to tell that voice of oppression, **"The blood speaks better things!"** When the Word tells you that you are NOW a child of the Living God (1st John 3:2) but the church, organized religion, and false humility tell you that you are a wretched sinner saved by grace; please scream at the top of your lungs**, "THE BLOOD SPEAKS BETTER THINGS!"**

Because our outside is so far from catching up with our inside, we are comfortable with thinking of ourselves as sinners. We do things with our minds and bodies which are definitely not righteous but because the Word says that we are saved by the cross; we take the ecclesiastical consolation prize. The religious compromise is a pacifier of sorts for our conscience. "Yes, amen, I am just a *sinner saved by grace.*" I have been saved by grace but because I misbehave at times and sin; I must still be a sinner, right? **Wrong!**

If you have received Jesus' rescue by agreeing with the Word that you are a sinner in need of a Savior and by believing enough that He was raised from the dead to say it out of your mouth; you have IMMEDIATELY become a child of the Living God. Your now a saint and a joint heir with Yeshua Jesus. Regardless of what you know about yourself or how you "feel" or what you think disqualifies you from being a child of the Living Father (John 6:57), the Word of God says that NOW BELOVED...YOU ARE A CHILD OF GOD! (1st John 3:1-2)

You are right with the Living God because of what Jesus has done to make you right. So, believing in what Jesus has done for you and accepting it results in Almighty God giving you the *Jesus Treatment*. (Romans 8:32/Ephesians 4:32) **You are not right with God because of what you have done**. All that we attempt to do (religious points) to "get right" with God mounts up to a pile of filthy rags according to Isaiah 64:6.

The devil knows you better than you know yourself! That is why he wants to keep you focused on what you used to do, what you used to be, where you came from, and what you just did that is not right. The evil thoughts and emotions you entertain at times to convince you that you are nothing more than a *sinner saved by grace.* Holy Scripture teaches no such thing as a sinner saved by grace.

Once we are *saved from sin by grace* the Word refers to us as saints and children of Almighty God. **Not sinners**. What scares the devil is the prospect of you and any believer diving into the Word and finding out what is right with you. What you are like in your resurrected spirit core. What God made right about you with *The* Cross. Once you find out that faith in The Cross has made you just like Jesus in your resurrected spirit core, you will (along with all believers who accept the revelation) finally set Jesus free to do what He's been wanting to do since He moved into your spirit core. He wants to do the same things through our bodies, which He did during His earthly ministry in His own body. But the devil wants us to focus on what we do wrong instead of putting confidence in the "*good work*" (Philippians 1:6) which Jesus has begun in us to make us right. We know beyond any shadow of doubt that we have come to Jesus and asked Him to forgive our sins and asked Him for a home in Heaven one day.

We also identify with the Apostle Paul when he says in Romans 7:18, "*For I know that in me (that is, in my flesh,) dwells no good thing*..." We cannot reconcile the two pictures we have of ourselves so we continue to slide down the rabbit hole of false humility believing we are simply sinners saved by grace. Lord have mercy!

Once we have accepted what Yeshua Jesus has done for us, the Word never again calls us sinners. **Religion does**. False humility does **but not the Word**. With that in mind, we have to realize that faith in the proper object of faith is very important.

Believing the *accuser of the believers* (Revelation 12:10) - the dark spirit - and agreeing with him regarding our identity is akin to Adam agreeing with the serpent in Eden. If you believe you are a sinner saved by grace then you have willingly handed over your true identity to the dark kingdom identity thief in exchange for an identity which is void of the Holy Spirit and fire.

Adam should have run the serpent out of the garden along with the devil the moment interaction with Havah/Eve started. Instead, he chose to observe the interaction rather than put an end to it. When we entertain that hellish thinking of being a *sinner saved by grace*, we observe and participate with the adversary and diminish the perception of our new identity as children of the Living God who has no sinners as children. Only the glorified righteous ones. (Romans 8:30)

Faith Contaminated?

THINK ABOUT IT! If we are still sinners to any degree in our resurrected (Romans 6:4/Ephesians 2:6) spirit core after being saved from sin by grace and made the righteousness of God; then Jesus' blood didn't go far enough. *The*

Cross did not do what was intended. That is essentially what we are saying when we gossip like that about our new identity. That subtle distinction is a veiled judgment against you to remind you of your failings and shortcomings. And to distract you from the true revelation of sanctification: The Cross made your spirit core perfect. (Hebrews 12:23) Eventually the rest of you will catch up. Jesus' righteousness is supposed to remind you of what He has made right with and about you but when you agree with that deception of *sinner saved by grace* you agree with your spiritual past. What WAS wrong with you and by implication what is wrong with you currently. In your resurrected spirit core, what is wrong with you? ABSOLUTELY NOTHING! We are commanded to condemn or disapprove of voices that pass judgment on us. (Isaiah 54:17) Instead, we tend to agree with the lies.

*No weapon that is formed against you shall prosper; and **every tongue** [voice] **that shall rise against you in judgment you shall condemn**. This is the heritage of the servants of the Lord, and their righteousness is of me, says the Lord.* Isaiah 54:17

Instead of soothing our conscience with false humility, we are expected to condemn those voices and speak what the *Spirit of Truth* speaks – the blood of Jesus. Our identity has been transformed by the Spirit of the Living God taking up residence in our resurrected spirit cores. To accept a false humility distorted identity to appease religious tradition and avoid feeling like a liar, we acquiesce to the deception and religious peer pressure. The eternal security of your soul is much more important that peer pressure. Let the Word be true and all other voices a liar. If you agree with the deception then what does that make you? Is God's love worth agreeing with rather than agreeing with the dark spirit? Check out this reminder:

13 Christ has redeemed us from the curse of the law, being made a curse for us: for it is written, Cursed is every one that hangs on a tree:
*14 That **the blessing of Abraham** might come on the Gentiles through Jesus Christ; that we might receive the promise of the Spirit through faith.*
Galatians 3:13-14

The blood of Jesus speaks, "*The Blessing of Abraham*" over every new creation believer. The blood of Jesus redeemed from the curse

(Galatians 3:13) every believer's life. We need to add faith to the blood and receive *The Blessing* and shun the curse. Jesus' blood shifted our spiritual, bodily, and financial paradigms from the curse to the universal cure. The charis [grace] of *The* Cross.

This is a good time to make the point that it is not the law that was cursed or is cursed. It is the breaking of the law that brings a curse. The law is so exacting and stringent that breaking one part of it made the violators guilty of breaking the whole law. Since Yeshua didn't break the law, He had to be cursed by a different route. Under the law, the instruction was given that bodies hanging on trees will be cursed by the Living God.(Deuteronomy 21:22-23) So, as Christian, let's be on solid theological ground regarding the law of Moses. Jesus said that He didn't come to do away with the law but to complete it. It is important for us not to believe something that is contrary to the clear teaching of the word of the Living God.

Yeshua Jesus became the curse so that we could become the blessing. He accepted or became sin so that we could become sinless [redeemed] and called the righteousness of the Living God. He was punished for our sin so that we could approach the presence of the Living

God boldly without trepidation or self consciousness. Or sin consciousness even. (Hebrews 9:9,14, 10:2,22) If we continue to walk in the light of the understanding of His precious blood and the grace covenant it purchased, we can fellowship with the Godhead as if we belong and guess what? We do...because of *The* Cross, the blood, and the name. We are justified by faith when we have more confidence in the Living God's goodness than in our badness or wrongness.

The Blood Speaks: You Are Righteous!

*For He has **made** him to be sin for us, who knew no sin; that we might be **made** the righteousness of God in him.*   2 Corinthians 5:21

IMPORTANT POINT: Why "*that we might be?*" Because the Most High God has done everything that needs to be done on His part to make us right with Him. To make us judgment proof. To give us the opportunity to trade our eternal death [thanks to Adam] for eternal life [thanks to Jesus' Cross, blood, and name]. Now it is your move. Now it is my move.

Yes, **right with God through faith** in *The* Cross even if you don't "feel" like it. Salvation, justification, redemption, etc are not established or confirmed by feelings but by faith in what the Word says. This is one of the simplest and most straight forward scriptures detailing our new identity in Christ but we don't really pay attention to it. We have to remember that every word in the Word of the Living God is important. It is absolutely important to slow down while reading the Word of God. Hang on every word and pay close attention. You might find more of your glory identity in the parentheses.

The Blood Speaks: You Are Justified!

23 Now it was not written for his sake alone, that it was imputed to him;
*24 But for us also, to whom it shall be imputed, if we believe on him that raised up **Jesus our Lord** from the dead;*
*25 Who was delivered for our offences, and **was raised again for our justification**.*

Romans 4:23-25

I used to think, and a few times taught, that the resurrection occurred so that we would know that can be justified. I thought the resurrection was a show for us. For our confidence. For our faith. That is true but there is so much more to the resurrection. The resurrection not only justifies the believer but also exonerates the Messiah. The princes of the kingdom of darkness condemned Our Lord to Hell because of the curse of hanging on a tree. (Deut. 21:22-23/Gal. 3:13) Because Jesus said that the debt had been paid in full ["it is finished"]; my reasoning for saying that Him being raised was only for our faith was that we were justified by Him dying on the cross. I later realized after much reasoning (Isaiah 1:18) and contemplation (Joshua 1:8) and reading the Word that the empty tomb is as important to His redemption mission as was the virgin birth. The furtherance of Christ's teachings and the restoration of the Jewish people depends on the resurrection. The resurrection wasn't symbolic. It was necessary for Jesus' exoneration. It is necessary for our faith and justification. A necessary anchor to the confidence of believers for ages to come.

The resurrection power of the Living God is on display when souls are saved, miracles are worked, bodies are healed, finances are blessed, brains are healed, minds are restored, and spontaneous charity is extended to the needy without them begging for it. Closer to the resurrection were the disciples which ran when Jesus was arrested. They hid behind locked doors when no one was after them. We need an anchor of faith to give us strength thousands of years after the resurrection. The disciples needed it even more. The disciples, also, needed something to give them the strength to endure and not run ever again as they did the night Messiah Yeshua was arrested in Gethsemane's garden. After the resurrection, those disciples never ran again. The never hid again.

Because the Jewish religious leaders rejected Yeshua as Messiah it opened the door for another nation or ethnics to be exposed to it and do so much more with it than the Jews ever have. But not ever will.

Therefore say I unto you, The kingdom of God shall be taken from you, and given to a nation bringing forth the fruits thereof. Matthew 21:43

Another nation [maybe a nation of Gentile believers?] will further the kingdom of the Living God in ways unheard of. The resurrection was a major "*selling point*" for Christianity. New creation believers have taken the resurrection and Jesus' cross to the four corners of the world and to the subcultures of every continent on the planet. Jesus' resurrection, I used to think and even taught once, occurred so that we would know that we are justified by His cross. By His redemption ministry.

As I have studied the promises, implications, and outcomes of *The* Cross; I have come to a more accurate conclusion. The resurrection is the capstone of the grace covenant. Jesus is the foundation and the cornerstone. His resurrection is the "Hear ye, hear ye," proclamation that the mission of *The* Cross was accomplished. Peace between God and man is possible. Peace between you and God is up to you. Take it!

I used to think that the resurrection was about our justification but that is only partially correct. Hebrews 1:6-9 appears to paint a picture of the resurrection. Jesus was brought **back into the world** [reborn?] by the Living God and received such a stamp of approval that Most High God said to Messiah Jesus, "*Your throne,* **Oh God***, is forever...*" Wait! The Living God called the God-Man...God? Yes, Emmanuel [God in an earth suit] and Prince of Peace received another title – God. Talk about a promotion!

Isaiah's prophecy ascribed many titles to the coming Savior of the world. One is Everlasting Father. Another is Mighty God. Isaiah's prophecy was so much more than clues. It clearly told us what the name of the Son and Child which would come *"shall be called..."* Because a name is a word, it is easy to conclude that the Word – Messiah Jesus – was predicted to be called *Mighty God* (Isaiah 9:6) and Hebrews harkens back to Psalm 45 to show that the resurrection was predicted as well.

No, the resurrection wasn't just for us but was also for Jesus. The resurrection was for the Innocent who gave up His rights, life, and justice for the Guilty. For us guilty. He accepted the nature of the serpent – the curse – which was the result of hanging on Calvary's tree. The Innocent died a criminal's death. Cursed or "cut off" was the result as Isaiah 53:8-10 and Daniel 9:26 refer. The Innocent was shamed by the onlookers who wagged their heads loathsomely at Him in disgust. He told those who were crying on cue for Him, "Don't cry for me but for yourselves," because the *Lamb of Redemption* would someday be the *Lion of Judgment.* And His cross would be the basis for that judgment.

He was fallen and all of Hell thought that He had failed His mission. All of Hell was convinced by their dark lord, "We got Him and mankind is ours to dominate forever and because He failed *I can exalt my throne above God's."* (Isaiah 14:13) Jesus' suffering in Hell was the equivalent of eternal punishment – IN OUR PLACE – but because the Innocent was sinless; Hell couldn't hold on to Him according to Acts 2:24.

But God released him from the horrors of death and raised him back to life, for death could not keep him in its grip.   Acts 2:24

Hell couldn't hold on to Him because He had no sinful actions or a sin nature weighing Him down. There was nothing inside Messiah Yeshua that belonged to the devil.(John 14:30)   He wasn't in Hell because of His own guilt (which there was none) but because of ours. Yours and mine. Once our sin nature and the trespasses were completely and thoroughly punished in Him, Christ was free. The curse, sin nature, iniquity, and trespasses were burned off Him nothing was left to hold Him down. It was time to rise.

3 The sorrows of death compassed me, and the pains of hell gat hold upon me: I found trouble and sorrow.
4 Then called I upon the name of the Lord; O Lord, I beseech thee, deliver my soul.
5 Gracious is the Lord, and righteous; yea, our God is merciful.

*6 The Lord preserves the simple: **I was brought low**, and he helped me.*
7 Return unto thy rest [ease/stasis], O my soul; for the Lord has dealt bountifully with thee.
8 For thou hast delivered my soul from death[the place of the dead], mine eyes from tears, and my feet from falling.[the fallen lifted up]
9 I will walk before the Lord in the land of the living. Psalms 116:3-9

The clues were there all along. "*I was brought low, you helped me, delivered my soul from death*," AND "*I will walk before the Lord in the land of the living or in my flesh*." What? I am dead but I will walk before Lord in my flesh? Jesus was on the cross quoting scripture and the criminals and soldiers heard Him. That is why one criminal called to Him, "Lord, remember me when you come into your kingdom," and a hardened Roman soldier said of Him, "Truly, this was the Son of God." That statement could cost a Roman soldier his life back then.

Do you think Messiah stopped quoting scripture in Hell? He, no doubt, quoted more. He was in the punishment of Hell quoting these and many other scriptures and finally His Father (and now our Father) said, "**Enough! The debt has been paid!**" Jesus' suffering didn't begin on the cross, though. He started sweating blood some nine to twelve hours earlier while praying in Gethsemane's garden. He was in redemption mode long before the arrest, the mock trials, and beatings started.

The Innocent was justified by His Father. The Innocent was justified for Himself. The Innocent was justified for the Guilty. For us. Because He was a substitute for us on many levels, He had to be resurrected not only for Himself but for us. We, by faith, are buried with Him (Romans 6:4) in judgment and raised with Him in *righteousness and true holiness* according to Ephesians 4:24. Messiah Jesus identified with our guilt so that we could identify with His innocence. With His righteousness. With His justification. He imputed – transferred - His perfection to our resurrected spirit core because He has the credentials to do just that. I mean...how amazing in this grace?

4 But God, who is rich in mercy, for his great love wherewith he loved us,
5 Even ***when we were dead in sins****, has quickened us* ***[resurrected us]*** *together with Christ, (by grace you are saved;)*
6 And has raised us up together, and made us sit together in heavenly places in Christ Jesus:

*7 That in the ages to come he might show the exceeding riches of **his grace** in his kindness **toward us** through Christ Jesus.*   Ephesians 2:4-7

The parenthesis of verse five are very telling. After saying that we are resurrected with Messiah Jesus, the verse tells us that we are saved by grace. What does that mean? Consider the distinction in conditions of the two parties which were resurrected. Christ's spiritual condition is a foregone conclusion – perfect and innocent. Our spirit condition, on the other hand, is spiritually dead in trespasses [deeds/violations] and sin [sin nature]without Him. We have no problem agreeing that Jesus – the Innocent - deserved to be resurrected. After all, He was innocent.

But us? We know that we deserved to remain spiritually dead. Amazing grace would turn us from dead to alive; but His grace is more than amazing. It is exceeding. It is more than we need. Not only were we rescued from death to life (John 5:24/1st John 3:14) but given so much more including part of His divine nature. From dead in trespasses in sin to partakers of the Living God's divine nature? Did we need that much grace to avoid Hell? That much grace has to be for something else. But what?

9...the mystery, which from the beginning of the world has been hid in God, who created all things by Jesus Christ:

10 To the intent that now **unto the principalities** *and powers in heavenly places* **might be known by the church** *the manifold wisdom of God,*

Ephesians 3:9b-10

Not only does the Living God want to show us what He can do with screwed up people, but He wants the rebellious spirits of the unseen realm to understand the majesty of His power. If He can do with us what He has, is, and will do; then what created spirit can think it can exalt itself above the author or creation? The exceeding grace is poured out on, in, and through us for the express purpose of one simple thing. God is showing off.

For the eyes of the Lord run to and fro throughout the whole earth, to show himself strong in the behalf of them **whose heart is perfect toward him**.   2 Chronicles 16:8a

After faith in The Cross, every new creation believer has a perfect heart/spirit core and the Living God wants to show off in the life of everyone who is willing to give Him the credit.

He wants to show off in your life. In my life. Even me. Now, that is amazing. The church has called this grace amazing but Ephesians 2:7 calls it exceeding. Over and above or more than we need. The grace of the Living God which rescues the sinner from the sin nature's appointment to be punished, is so much more grace than we need to be exempted from judgment.

We are not only rescued from judgment by grace, but we are also put in a legally secure position of being declared righteous, justified, and sanctified by the *Righteous Judge of Creation*. "Amazing" is to be rescued from eternal punishment. "Exceeding" is to be added to the family and given the right to personally fellowship with the Godhead with the Holy Spirit residing inside our new creation spirit core.

It shouldn't be difficult for you to understand why I reasoned that the work of *The* Cross was so effective that justification was an inevitable outcome. The problem with my previous reasoning was that proclamations of justification, righteousness, and imputed perfection void of indisputable evidence would amount to nothing more than a whimsical wish. An ecclesiastical pipe dream.

"Where's the evidence?" That's the eternal question plaguing the work of the gospel if there were no resurrection. The evidence of the resurrection is indisputable. Writings from Middle Eastern historians of the first and second centuries are replete with resurrection related accounts. You will not have any problems finding some anti-Christ documentaries supposedly proving that there is no evidence of the historical Jesus.

Some even say that certain first century historians who confirmed the life and resurrection of Yeshua Jesus have been disproved. Simply do your own research especially from non Christian sources.

From Flavius Josephus about 93 A.D.

About this time there lived Jesus, a wise man, if indeed one ought to call him a man. For he was one who performed surprising deeds and was a teacher of such people as accept the truth gladly. He won over many Jews and many of the Greeks. He was the Messiah. And when, upon the accusation of the principal men among us, Pilate had condemned him to a cross, those who had first come to love him did not cease. He appeared to them spending a *third day restored to life*, for the prophets of God had foretold these things and a thousand other marvels about him. And the tribe of the Christians, so called after him, has still to this day not disappeared.

Jewish Antiquities, 18.3.3 §63ᵛ

Pliny the Younger's Letters to Emperor Trajan

Roman magistrate nicknamed, Pliny the Younger, wrote to Trajan regarding his dealings with Christians. Pliny speaks of "interrogating" them two and three times threatening them with punishment. Those who wouldn't denounce that Messiah Jesus was risen were ordered executed. Pliny also informs Trajan that Roman citizens which wouldn't denounce Jesus were shipped to Rome. (for further interrogation no doubt) Pliny mentioned that those who were really Christians wouldn't curse Christ. [as the former or fake ones had?]

13 You were dead because of your sins and because your sinful nature was not yet cut away. Then God made you alive with Christ, for he forgave all our sins.
14 He canceled the record of the charges against

us and took it away by nailing it to the cross.
*15 In this way, **he disarmed the spiritual rulers
and authorities**.[of the kingdom of darkness] **He
shamed them publicly** [stripped them of their
power] by his victory over them on the cross.*

Colossians 2:13-15

"Shaming them publicly" refers to the customary *Trump Processional* in which the kings and generals of the defeated forces were paraded in front of the citizens of the victorious force. The term *trump* is simply an abbreviated version of the word *triumphant*. Because Jesus trumped the forces of darkness on their own battlefield, He paraded them in humility before the amphitheater of the universe.

Jesus shamed the author of shame. The dark spirit and all of his minions were shamed by *The* Cross. They attempted to shame, enslave, and destroy Jesus for being on the cross but they simply could not keep Him in their grasps according to Acts 2:24. The curse and all but Jesus held shame in contempt according to Hebrews 12:2. He disesteemed shame and even nailed that to His cross. *The* Cross has handled shame once and for all so forget what you used to be and if you do sin then confess it at the throne of grace and repent from your heart and forget it...along with the shame.

The Living God resurrected Messiah Jesus to publicly justify Him before the entire unseen realm. The principalities and powers of darkness were put on notice that they had illegally imprisoned the innocent Son of God. His indisputable innocence meant that He would justifiably be resurrected. Because He was punished and died on behalf of us guilty others, then we would enjoy the benefits of His exoneration. Jesus' exoneration would equate to our justification.

The Son of God was gloriously victorious. Jesus marched the generals of darkness out on the dais of the universe and TOOK the keys to death, Hell, and the grave. His reward included all power and authority bestowed upon Him when the Living God called Him God.(Hebrews 1:8) It stuns me every time I hear it. The sin nature would no longer dominate humanity.

The only thing required to enjoy the benefits of righteousness, justification, and sanctification is faith in what Jesus did before, on, and after *The* Cross. Jesus referenced the ease with which one can be transformed from a sinner to a saint when he spoke of Moses' brass serpent in John 3:14.

14 And as Moses lifted up the serpent in the wilderness, even so must the Son of man be lifted up:
15 That whosoever believes in him should not perish, but have eternal life.　　　John 3:14-15

8 And the Lord said unto Moses, Make thee a fiery serpent, and set it upon a pole: and it shall come to pass, that every one that is bitten, when he looks upon it, shall live.
9 And Moses made a serpent of brass, and put it upon a pole, and it came to pass, that if a serpent had bitten any man, when he beheld the serpent of brass, he lived.　　　Numbers 21:8-9

For those with the serpent's venom (sin nature?) coursing through their veins, all they needed to do to recover or be rescued from the deadly venom was to look at the brass serpent and they would instantly be healed. Just look and live? Yes, and Jesus related His redemption ministry to that situation. Can you imagine some naysayers writhing in pain from the venom's damaging effects saying, "I don't see how simply looking at a brass serpent will recover me from this venom," as they look up? Before they finished the sentence, they experienced instantaneous healing. I imagine their words trailing off and they never completed the sentence. They weren't instructed to believe it would work but only to do it. And it worked! Putting faith in Jesus' cross is that effortless. Why? Because even the faith isn't your own. He gives you that also.

For by grace are you saved through faith; and that not of yourselves: it is the gift of God:

Ephesians. 2:8

Yes, **even the faith to believe for the grace is given to us** by the Living God. How amazing is that? He gives us the faith which opens up the power of the resurrection to us. I used to think that the Living God could have justified us by legal decree which He did but He refused to do it without an evidentiary foundation. The resurrection is the foundation. The public resurrection is the evidence.

The fact that the disciples couldn't be intimidated by threats of torture or death just forty or so days after the crucifixion is circumstantial evidence that something happened between the time of them running when Jesus was arrested and them never running again. The only thing which makes sense is that the accounts of the resurrection are true. John was the only one which stayed close to Jesus throughout His arrest, trials, beatings, and crucifixion. He believed or knew something which the others didn't. He was the one closest to the Master during His ministry. He was also the one disciple which died of natural causes over sixty five years after the resurrection. Why?

Our Heavenly Father made the resurrection of His Son an undeniable display. Historical writings by non-Christian Roman historians and others validate many accounts of the life of Jesus. His resurrection is a matter of record for the Jewish leaders which manipulated the Romans to kill Him. The Living God made sure that the resurrection would be an undeniable historical fact which cannot be dismissed by the antagonist/agnostic adage, "If you believe the Bible." The resurrection didn't happen in the Bible. It was recorded in the Bible that the resurrection happened in Jerusalem. The Living God wants it to be crystal clear to us and the spiritually dead that faith in Jesus' cross is based on a historical fact. Whether you believe it or not.

1 Therefore being justified by faith, we have peace with God through our Lord Jesus Christ:

*2 By whom also we have access by faith into **this grace wherein we stand**, and rejoice in hope of the glory of God.*   Romans 5:1-2

This Covenant of Grace in which and on which we stand is a sure foundation. The adversary is relentless in attempting to keep believers off balance on the shaky footing of religion and false humility and distracted from the facts. The resurrection is a historical fact. Our access into this grace covenant is just as concrete. Justification is ours. Sanctification is ours. Redemption is ours. It is important to remember that we are not simply justified by Jesus' cross, blood or sacrifice. We are justified **by putting faith in those things**. Faith is an act [action] of the will and the Living God will not violate the free will of any individual.

Faith is an act and that is why Jesus said that believing in the One the Father sent is the "*working*" of the works of the Living God. That's right...not just justified by the cross but justified by faith in *The* Cross. If Dame Isabel Piczek is correct, Jesus' resurrection [made possible by His cross] scrubbed the universe clean and transformed it "*as far as the curse of sin is found.*" [from *Joy To The World* hymn] Simply putting faith in Jesus' cross also scrubs clean the eternity which is inside our spirit core.

We need to be justified by faith because we can't trust our feelings. Faith is connected to the inner spirit core and connects us directly to the Living God. Feelings are as fickle as a windsock and make a shaky foundation for confidence. With feelings you never "feel" saved, redeemed, righteous, justified or eternally secure but with faith that comes from the Word of the Living God [faith is founded on facts] you know that you are saved. You know that you are right with the Living God. You know that you are justified. You know that you are exactly what the mirror of His word says you are. What a mighty, marvelous, and wonderful Living God we serve!

9 Know you not that the unrighteous shall not inherit the kingdom of God? Be not deceived: neither fornicators, nor idolaters, nor adulterers, nor effeminate, nor abusers of themselves with mankind,
10 Nor thieves, nor covetous, nor drunkards, nor revilers, nor extortionist, shall inherit the kingdom of God.
*11 And such **were some of you**: but you **are washed**, but you **are sanctified**, but you **are justified** in the name of the Lord Jesus, and by the Spirit of our God.* 1 Corinthians 6:9-11

We know that those behaviors don't change overnight unless the Living God has done a special work in you to get you on your way sooner than later. Some people, after having their moment with Jesus, never return to drugs, prostitution or gossip ever again. In some cases, the Living God has some special ministry or endeavor in store for such people. Either way, the accurate understanding of grace, sanctification, and justification is critical to all believers. Let's take a look at that 11th verse in a different way:

*And such **were** some of you:*
*but **the blood speaks**, "you **are washed**"*
*but **the blood speaks**, "you **are sanctified**"*
*but **the blood speaks**, "you **are justified**"*
in the name of the Lord Jesus, and by the Spirit of our God.

It is interesting that the Word says to the believers that you WERE those things implying that everything has changed but if we are honest about our spiritual walk without being disrespectful of the Word, those behaviors are dogged when it comes to sticking around. If we understand the process of sanctification, we know that those old behaviors can be triggered and we fall into them if we don't guard our hearts and motivations.

Until our outside even begins the process of catching up with the inside we might find ourselves engaging in those behaviors which Yeshua Jesus saved us out of. The good news is that we can look into the mirror of God's word and find out what we have become on the inside where the real us resides along with our spirit core roommate - the Holy Spirit. Yes, we have engaged in wrong behavior but that doesn't mean that *The* Cross didn't take. It simply means that we are still in a body of flesh.

The Word here says that regardless of what you are struggling with on the outside, remember that you have been washed, sanctified, and justified AT THE CORE where it is most important. Jesus criticized the religious leaders who pretended to be right on the outside while their insides were full of death. "*Dead men's bones,*" Jesus said in Matthew 23:27.

We have had our inside flooded with the Zoë (John 10:10) life of the Living God through His Spirit when the Living God said inside us as He did in Genesis, "Light be," and that light which Adam turned off with his betrayal was turned back on by *The* Cross. So, on the inside we are full of life but our outside seems to be just about the same as it was before we got saved. Still, that is loads better than being dead on the inside and pretending to be spiritually alive like the religious leaders of Jesus' day. What about the religious leaders of today?

A preacher can consider how full his or her schedule is and, in despair, can take their own life. Another preacher can have an even busier schedule and look for more things to do. The difference between the two is the first is spiritually dead on the inside running on soul power and the second is full of the Spirit of the Living God allowing the Spirit to live through them. Soul power is finite but the Spirit of the Living God is infinite. A preacher can run on soul power or the power of the Spirit. The former is a shallow puddle compared the endless depths of the latter.

Jesus called the religious leaders with the dead spirit core hypocrites because they were broken pretending to be fixed. What would you call fixed people pretending to be broken? What would you call saints convinced that they are *still sinners BUT saved by grace*? What would you call those who have been made righteous opening public prayer with, "We are not worthy," and others saying, "amen," in agreement? Is that the blind [to righteousness] leading the blind to a ditch?

Awake to righteousness...   1 Corinthians 15:34a

I say, "The blood speaks better things!"   The same cross which saves and justifies the sinner also sanctifies the saint.   We have to teach our people to see themselves the way the Word teaches us of ourselves. And stop using the lenses of false humility. We also have to study for ourselves and stop getting all of our Bible learning from others.   We have to learn firsthand the voice of Jesus' blood.

The Blood Speaks: Paid In Full!

13 And you, being dead in your sins and the uncircumcision [covenant outsiders] of your flesh, has he quickened together with him, having forgiven you all trespasses;
14 Blotting out the handwriting of ordinances that was against us, which was contrary to us, and took it out of the way, nailing it to his cross;

Colossians 2:13-14

The Blood Speaks: Imputed Perfection!

10 By the which will we are sanctified through the offering of the body of Jesus Christ once for all.

11 And every priest stands daily ministering and offering oftentimes the same sacrifices, which can never take away sins:

*12 But this man, after he had offered <u>one sacrifice for sins forever</u>, **sat down** on the right hand of God;*

"Sat down" means mission accomplished

13 From hereafter expecting till his enemies be made his footstool.

*14 For by one offering he **has perfected for ever** them that are sanctified.*

15 Whereof the Holy Ghost also is a witness to us: for after that he had said before,

16 This is the covenant that I will make with them after those days, says the Lord, I will put my laws into their hearts, and in their minds will I write them;

17 And their sins and iniquities will I remember no more. Hebrews 10:10-17

So, if you fall into sin but your "want to" got saved when you did then just remember that **the blood speaks better things** and just get back up, rush to the throne of grace, ask forgiveness, obtain mercy, dust yourself off, and get back to fellowship and sharing. When you need your Heavenly Father to be the God of a 2nd, 3rd, or 100th chance but the voices of the dark realm are telling you that it's too late for you; remember that the blood of Jesus speaks better things and keep in mind that you feeling bad about doing bad means you have a conscience.

Did you have a conscience before meeting Messiah Yeshua? Did you feel bad about doing wrong before coming to Christ? If so, not for long. Having a conscience after meeting Jesus is a good indication that your "want to" got saved along with you. When it does, you can't be comfortable with sin. When it does, you can no longer be the nasty person running new people out of the church. Did your "want to" get saved?

When it does, you run that gossip demon out of your life. Just as David encouraged himself (Isaiah 30:6) when his entire force considered turning on him, you keep in mind that the blood of Jesus speaks better things and use that and the words which the blood speaks to lift your spirits.

The encouraging words of Jesus' blood are:

Justified
Sanctified
Redeemed
Child of the Living God
Forgiven
Blessed

Graced
Mercy

If it be possible, as much as [resides] in you, live peaceably with all men. Romans 12:18

The Word of God is called the *incorruptible seed* according to 1st Peter 1:23. Is it possible that all that I have put forth so far has the element of seed in it? By that I am asking if the Living God puts the kingdom inside us as big as it is but in seed or germinating form that we have to cultivate and grow? I don't know the answer but I think I know the question. Something about rush hour traffic brought this verse to mind yesterday and I saw it for the first time as a challenge to stretch myself. How do you know how much is in you? How do you measure it? By pushing pass your breaking and boiling points the next time or deciding what they are beforehand?

How can you gauge your capacity for life's challenges? In light of the reasoning set forth so far in this book, does it mean that if I keep in mind what has been done in me by *The* Cross of Yeshua that I will consciously stretch myself to endure more and more slights, attacks, and struggles? If that is the case then if I want to prove that good, acceptable, and perfected will of the Living God regarding me, I will endure more in the present situation than I did in the previous one. Each time I will increase my capacity with the help of the Holy Spirit and with the personal challenge to become what I have already been made by the power of *The* Cross. Just a thought I wanted to share.

CHAPTER FIVE

HAVE YOUR SINS BEEN FORGIVEN?

*All we like sheep have gone astray; We have turned, every one, to his own way; And **the Lord has laid on Him the iniquity of us all**. Yet **it pleased the Lord to bruise Him**; He has put Him to grief. When You make His soul an offering for sin, He shall see His seed, He shall prolong His days, And the pleasure of the Lord shall prosper in His hand.*

Isaiah 53:6,10

The answer is yes, yes, yes IF you have asked the Almighty for forgiveness of your sins and accepted the Lordship of Yeshua Jesus who died in your place on your cross and took your punishment for sin. (2ND Corinthians 5:21) Don't base your response to this question on how you "FEEL" about yourself but on what God's Word says about you. The Almighty judged and punished the sins of us all in Jesus on *The* Cross and for us to take advantage of that atoning marvel we simply need to tell the LORD Almighty that we accept Jesus' cross, blood, and name for the payment of our sin debt and thank HIM for it.

In the 53rd chapter of his prophecy, Isaiah gives a cryptic account of extreme suffering. It appears that an individual is being wounded, crushed, bruised, chastised, and punished in atrocious ways. The 10th verse tells us that the Lord bruises this individual and was actually "pleased" to do so. Backing up to the 6th verse, we find that ALL the iniquity of everyone who ever have lived and ever will live was laid on Yeshua Jesus. "*Punishment for sin*" is one of the interlinear definitions given for the word "*iniquity.*" Another definition is "*fault.*" We were at fault because of our sin nature but Jesus took the punishment. Thank you Jesus!

We eventually learn that the predicted suffering was referring to the Messiah – Yeshua

Jesus. The suffering person being referred to was the Messiah. God's wrath – judgment - punishment on the sin nature as well as sinful acts of the past, present, and future was poured out on crucifixion day. The debt was paid but not by Adam who was responsible for sin being introduced into the world and the sin nature being introduced into the human race. That debt wasn't paid by any of Adam's descendants who inherited his sin nature. Because of the inherited sin nature, all of Adam's descendants were born guilty and spiritually dead. That is definitely being born the wrong way.

The great news of the gospel is that the same effort which we personally expended to become sinners –nothing – can make us righteous.

18 Therefore, as through one man's offense judgment came to all men, resulting in condemnation, even so through one Man's righteous act the free gift came to all men, resulting in justification of life.
19 For as by one man's disobedience **many were made sinners**, *so also by one Man's obedience* **many will be made righteous**. Romans 5:18-19

The Old Testament sacrificial system pointed forward to *The* Cross of the Messiah which would take away the sin nature and pay the debt which the Living God's holy nature demanded. Sin and the sin nature could not be ignored. God had to pass judgment on it but THANKS BE TO GOD that Jesus agreed to take the punishment in our place.(Hebrews 10:5) Just as the innocent animals were sacrificed to cover the sins of the people and nation under the Old Covenant; Jesus, the Innocent, agreed to be sacrificed on the altar of *The* Cross. For some reason, His Father who is now our Father was pleased to sacrifice Jesus.

yet it pleased the Lord to bruise him; he has put him to grief: Isaiah 53:10a

What reason would the Living God have for being pleased to punish His Son? His innocent Son? **That reason is you**. That reason is me. Punishing Jesus was the most important part of the rescue plan. That plan was implemented by the Living God's Agape Love. Jesus was also pleased to stand between us and God's judgment and punishment on sin and the sin nature.

*For it was fitting for Him, for whom are all things and by whom are all things, **in bringing many sons to glory**, to make the captain of their*

salvation perfect through sufferings.

Hebrews 2:10

We do this by keeping our eyes on Jesus, the champion who initiates and perfects our faith. Because of **the joy awaiting him**, *he endured the cross, disregarding its shame. Now he is seated in the place of honor beside God's throne.*

Hebrews 12:2 NLT

"*Because of the joy to come*," the Innocent endured the cross thinking nothing of the shame [being cursed of God and crucified naked]. What was the joy to come? You in the family of God! Me in the family of God! Holy Scripture teaches in 1st John that we have fellowship with the godhead because of the blood of Jesus.

6 If we say that we have fellowship with him, and walk in darkness, we lie, and do not the truth:
*7 But if we walk in the light, as he is in the light, we have **fellowship one with another**, and the blood of Jesus Christ his Son cleanses us from all sin.* 1 John 1:6-7

Is verse seven here saying that continually walking in the light results in continual impartation of Jesus' perfection? Continual impartation of Jesus' righteousness and justification keeps us clean and worthy to enter the fellowship circle with the Godhead. That sounds fanciful but it also sounds scriptural.

When I look at verse seven in the manuscript version I see, "*mutual fellowship one with the others.*" The "*others*" could be referring to the two persons mentioned in a few earlier verses. Verse 1 mentions the Word of Life which we know is Jesus. Verse 2 mentions the Father. Verse 2 actually mentions fellowshipping with the Father and His Son Yeshua Jesus. Verse 5 mentions God and then verse six says walking in darkness [false teaching and unrepentant sin] precludes us from fellowship with the Father and Son. And then...if we remain in the light [of the Word of Life] [of accurate teaching and repenting when we sin] we will have mutual fellowship with the three members of the Godhead. The only thing keeping us in fellowship with the Father and the Messiah Son is the blood of Jesus constantly cleansing us from all sin. WOW!

Just as the blood of Jesus cleanses us at salvation to put us in the family of God, the continual honoring of His sacrifice through needed repentance and forgiveness cleanses us continually and forever. All because the Innocent was published in our stead. Yes, an innocent was punished in lieu of the guilty.

Listen to what Isaiah 53:4-9 says about the Innocent:

He endured the suffering that should have been **OURS***; the pain that* **we should have borne***.*

All the while we thought that his suffering was punishment sent by God.

He bore **our sins** *in His body on the tree*

But because of **OUR sins** *he was wounded, beaten because of the evil we were, did, and would do.* **We are healed** *by the punishment he suffered, made whole by the blows he received.*

All of us *were like sheep that were lost,* **each of us** *going his own way.*

But the Lord made our punishment fall on Him, the punishment **all of us deserved***.*

He was treated harshly, but endured it humbly; he never said a word.

Like a lamb about to be slaughtered, like a sheep

about to be sheared, he never said a word.

He was arrested and sentenced and led off to die, and no one cared about his fate.

*He was put to death for **the sins of [OTHER]** people.*

He was placed in a grave with evil men, he was buried with the rich, even though...he had never committed a crime or ever told a lie."   TEV

The language of the first chapter of the book of Hebrews indicates some sort of celebration and possible promotion or exultation of the Innocent. It falls in line with the second chapter of Philippians.

*9 Wherefore **God also has highly exalted him**, and given him a name which is above every name: 10 That at the name of Jesus every knee should bow, of things in heaven, and things in earth, and things under the earth; 11 And that every tongue should confess that Jesus Christ is Lord, to the glory of God the Father.*
                                        Philippians 2:9-11

The Innocent did not deserve the curse but

He needed to hang on Calvary's tree so that the curse would come. The curse resulted in Him accepting the nature of the serpent –the sin nature – so that the Living God could punish sin once and for all putting aside the animal sacrifices of the Old Covenant.

The shedding of blood covered sins and sealed contracts in the Old Testament. After reading James Lee Beall's Christian catechism, *Laying the Foundation: Achieving Christian Maturity*, one could safely and accurately conclude that grace is the name of the New Covenant which was purchased by the blood of the sacrificed Messiah. Because this covenant is signed in the blood of Jesus, His name has been elevated in authority above every other name in existence. Hebrews chapter one paints the picture, though, of Him being promoted to the pinnacle of the universe in authority.

5 For God never said to any angel what he said to Jesus: "You are my Son. Today I have become your Father." God also said, "I will be his Father, and he will be my Son."
6 And when he brought his firstborn Son into the world, God said, "Let all of God's angels worship him."
7 Regarding the angels, he says, "He sends his

angels like the winds, his servants like flames of fire."

*8 But **to the Son he says, "Your throne, O God**, endures forever and ever. You rule with a scepter of justice.*

9 You love justice and hate evil. Therefore, O God, your God has anointed you, pouring out the oil of joy on you more than on anyone else."
10 He also says to the Son, "In the beginning, Lord, you laid the foundation of the earth and made the heavens with your hands.
11 They will perish, but you remain forever.

Hebrews 1:5-11a NLT

When God calls you, "God," I guess you just got promoted. On Resurrection Day, the Living God promoted the God-Man – Immanuel – Jesus - Yeshua – to the position of God. Did He simply return to the position He held previously? Either way the name of Jesus [Greek for His Hebrew name Yeshua] is now the most powerful name in existence. Even before *The* Cross, He shared His authority with the disciples and demons were cast out of the oppressed. Before *The* Cross, the sick were healed via His shared authority. After *The* Cross, He has taken up residence in the spirit core of every new creation believer and brought the authority of His matchless name with Him.

He has done everything He needed to do to get us right with God again and has gone exceedingly abundantly beyond that to give us all things which pertain to life and godliness including downloading His Spirit, Name, Word, and presence into our spirit core. He endured the hell of crucifixion and has earned the right to judge. The fifth chapter of John quotes Jesus saying that the Father God has delegated judgment to the Son.

22 Moreover, the Father judges no one, but has entrusted all judgment to the Son,
23 that all may honor the Son just as they honor the Father. He who does not honor the Son does not honor the Father, who sent him. John 5:22-23

The Cross is the basis for judgment day because The Innocent has already been judged for your sins and suffered greatly to pay the price for any "*guilty*" who will accept it. You can face God based on Jesus' merit and works or you can take the other option and face judgment day on your own merit. Not a good idea.

If anyone's merit other than Jesus' could have satisfied the debt then Jesus' suffering was not necessary. Jesus is the way to the Father. If you think that **all roads lead to God** then you are correct. **Only in judgment** though. Yes, all roads lead to God in judgment. There is, however, one road which leads to God in righteousness – JESUS. Putting faith in His cross is the only way to be at peace with God.

In *The* Cross, your sins have already been judged and paid for in Jesus. On your own...well...you are lost. The sixth chapter of Revelation says that some people will be so anti Jesus [against the only way for peace with God] that they will pray for falling rocks to kill them rather than acknowledge the designer of the heavens and the earth. Still, it is extremely important to understand that Jesus' cross is judgment day for the new creation believer.

Judgment day is not simply some cataclysmic event in distant future. According to the World Health Organization, about 56 million people die every year. That means that *judgment day* comes every day for over 150,000 people around the world. You can have judgment day at *The* Cross or at the throne of God. *The* Cross is much more favorable because your sins are already judged in Yeshua Jesus. The sad thing is that some will so hate God's way that they will pray for death rather than mercy.

15 And the kings of the earth, and the great men, and the rich men, and the chief captains, and the mighty men, and every bondman, and every free man, hid themselves in the dens and in the rocks of the mountains;

*16 And said to the mountains and rocks, Fall on us, and hide us from the face of him that sits on the throne, and from **the wrath of the Lamb:***

17 For the great day of his wrath is come; and who shall be able to stand? Revelation 6:15-17

Notice verse sixteen? The wrath of the Lamb? He was the **Lamb of Redemption** during His first coming and will be the **Lion of Judgment** when He returns. Go back through the gospels and see that Jesus did not condemn or judge people even when they were clearly sinful. He was so focused on the purpose of His first coming that nothing distracted Him from grace filled moments. After the accusers of the adulterous woman dropped their stones and walked away in shame; Jesus said to the lady, "Neither do I condemn you BUT sin no more." Why? Next time He won't be a sacrifice but a judge.

Is it possible that the Father has delegated all judgment to the Son because the Son was judged for all of our sins, all of my sins, all of your sins? The Living God punished all our sins already in Jesus so He is the perfect Judgment Day adjudicator.

The **Cross is the best, only,** and legitimate basis for Judgment Day and not good works, nice behavior or even religious deeds.

Okay, but doesn't the Bible say that we should do something to help others along the way [to Heaven I suppose] and especially the unfortunate and those who may never be able to return the favor? Jesus did say that doing this kind of stuff for the "least" of society is just like doing it for Him. If that is the case then shouldn't those good works "get us in?" Let's take a closer look at that portion of scripture in light of the what we are learning about the covenant called grace.

34 "Then the King will say to those on his right, 'Come, you who are blessed by my Father; take your inheritance, the kingdom prepared for you since the creation of the world.
35 For I was hungry and you gave me something to eat, I was thirsty and you gave me something to drink, I was a stranger and you invited me in,
36 I needed clothes and you clothed me, I was sick

and you looked after me, I was in prison and you came to visit me.'

37 "Then the righteous will answer him, 'Lord, when did we see you hungry and feed you, or thirsty and give you something to drink?

38 When did we see you a stranger and invite you in, or needing clothes and clothe you?

39 When did we see you sick or in prison and go to visit you?'

*40 "The King will reply, 'I tell you the truth, whatever you did for one of the least of **these brothers of mine**, you did for me.'*

41 "Then he will say to those on his left, 'Depart from me, you who are cursed, into the eternal fire prepared for the devil and his angels.

42 For I was hungry and you gave me nothing to eat, I was thirsty and you gave me nothing to drink,

43 I was a stranger and you did not invite me in, I needed clothes and you did not clothe me, I was sick and in prison and you did not look after me.'

44 "They also will answer, 'Lord, when did we see you hungry or thirsty or a stranger or needing clothes or sick or in prison, and did not help you?'

Matthew 25:34-44 NIV

In some churches, reading more than five verses results in losing the attention of most but

I will take the risk. Remember, these are my observations and probably quite different than what you have heard before but keep an open and vigilant mind just in case there may be some meat on these bones. Okay, the main point I think Jesus is addressing is indifference. I used to think that hate was the opposite of God's Agape Love until I heard a teaching on the global Catholic TV network explaining hate and indifference. You can look up the definition for yourself but I am sure you already know what it is. The story of the Good Samaritan is a perfect example.

The Good Samaritan was the only one in the story who was not indifferent to the plight of the victim. All the others didn't hate the victim. They just didn't care one way or another what would become of him. The indifferent all had their personal reasons for ignoring the victim. Those reasons included ceremonial restrictions. And some, no doubt, were late for very important dates. Interruptions were not allotted for. Who were Jesus' brothers? The Jews! Indifference towards the Jewish people and Israel is extremely dangerous. Life and death! Israel and the Jewish people are important to the Most High God and critical to the well being of the world.

Indifference is worst than hate. To ignore the suffering of others is evil and damnable according to this scripture but let's dig a little deeper where Jesus is speaking of visiting the sick, imprisoned, and giving food and clothing. Jesus always taught on multiple levels at one time. When He is talking about giving the hungry food is it possible that He is speaking of the food that feeds the spirit and soul? I know, some say that it is detrimental to, "be so Heavenly minded that you can become no earthly good," but if you pay any attention to the Word you should conclude that the time on earth is a puff of smoke compared to eternity.

With that in mind, doesn't it make sense that spiritual food is more important than natural food? Sounds strange coming from a stout individual like myself. Anyway, if we are not walking in love; we are walking in something else. But what? Let's see 1 John 2:9-11:

*9 He that says he is in the light, and **hates his brother**, **is in darkness** even until now.*
*10 He that **loves his brother abides in the light**, and there is none occasion of stumbling in him.*
*11 But he that **hates his brother is in darkness**, and walks in darkness, and knows not whither he goes, because that darkness has blinded his eyes.*

So, walking in anything other than love is walking in darkness. Indifference is darkness. Hate is darkness. Indifference is more damaging because we can be indifferent even about the gospel. When Jesus is talking about clothing those in need is it possible that the most important clothing is eternal clothing? Well, what's that? Righteousness maybe? The clear understanding/revelation that *The* Cross clothes us in the righteousness of Jesus IS DESIGNED TO give us peace and calm in the presence of the Living God. Even IF we do commit sin, we come boldly [RUSH WITHOUT HESITATION OR FEAR] to the throne of grace to obtain mercy and find grace for us and us only. After salvation, God's hands are untied in our lives. Rushing to repent after becoming believers is to cleanse us and our conscience so that it won't get in the way of us praising, praying, and approaching our Living Father. Our Loving Father.

The proper teaching of the grace covenant secured by Jesus' cross paints the picture of the new creation believer as well as slaves of religion being dressed with the imputed perfection of the Lamb. Jesus' perfection is bestowed on (1st John 3:1) the believer and the believer is dressed in robes of righteousness because Jesus became sin for the ungodly (Romans 4:5) so that the ungodly **might** BE MADE the righteousness of the Living God in Yeshua Jesus.

Yes, we are made the righteousness and not just righteous BUT MADE the righteousness. I don't know exactly what that means but I like thinking that it is multiple layered. Also, have you read anywhere in the Bible where the Living God UNMADE anything? Sounds like some eternal clothing. Everlasting even.

IF what I am asserting here is accurate then the difference between the righteous and the damned is what they did with the gospel of grace. I know it might seem like I am splitting hairs but don't you know that the Living God pays such close attention to you that even the very hairs on your head are accounted for. That means that he also knows your motivations and emotions regardless of your stoic expression. Yes, let's feed the poor, clothe the naked, and not ignore the least of these but let's not do it thinking that is what it takes to get in.

You could help the poor every day of your life with a smile on your face and bitterness in your heart because it seems to have no end. You can speak in front of a group of seniors at an underprivileged assisted living facility and they all leave thinking, "What a great person," all the while you're thinking," I hope this is enough to get me in." An old Christian "spiritual" song goes, "*May the works I've done speak for me,*" which is a silent sentiment of many. We have to be sure that the object of our faith is correct. Only two works will speak for us and get us in.

1   The work Jesus completed on the cross
2   Us putting faith in Him and that work

28 Then said they unto him, What shall we do, that we might work the works of God?
*29 Jesus answered and said unto them, This is **the work of God, that you believe** on him whom he has sent.*   John 6:28-29

Spiritual food that never spoils and eternal clothing that never tatters is so much more important than a hot bowl of soup and a sweater. Learning the covenant of grace and giving it away in droves is eternally important. **Charity with an eternal purpose is my point**. What good is a full belly to a lost soul? What good are good works if your soul is lost? If you want to throw the dice and face Judgment Day on your own merits then that is the dumbest thing I have ever heard. Wouldn't it make more sense to take your preemptive Judgment Day appointment at the foot of *The* Cross based on the merits of the One who already passed the test and secured grace for you? Or do would you prefer to try to work for something which Jesus has already earned for you? Isn't it obvious which is the sure thing?

A prominent politician was quoted saying, ["There has to be a place for me in Heaven with all I have done for the less fortunate."] Do you think this person's faith for admission into Heaven in the right place? Should the object of their faith be Jesus' work for them or their work for others? The work which they have done or faith in the work which Jesus has already done and passed with throne promoting colors? There is only one right answer and you know which one it is. We want to "do" something to contribute to our salvation. Jesus said that the most important work we can do is to believe.

On the previous page, the reference from the sixth chapter of John's gospel is quite telling. The religious leaders were comfortable jumping through religious hoops and dangling the *carrot and stick* of absolution before others to get them to do the same. They wanted to contribute to their righteousness with God. If they, I or you could contribute to our own righteousness wouldn't it cease to be the righteousness of God? Jesus told His inquirers that the only work the

Living God would accept from us [in regard to eternal security and rescue from judgment] is faith.

Yeah, but that's not enough work is it? The 11th chapter of John's gospel could be called *The Gospel According to Lazarus*. It is amazing how the Living God uses actual events as spiritual metaphors. If Lazarus represents broken humanity dead in trespasses and sins then how does he find salvation or spiritual life? He doesn't. The Living God [in Christ reconciling the lost to Himself] does all the work. The only thing Lazarus had to do was nothing. When you compare what Jesus has done for us to what we do [believe in faith] to benefit from it you conclude that we do nothing. The dead cannot cry for help. The Living One simply comes and rescues us.

Many will reject God's way because it is too easy. "Why can't I contribute to my own salvation?" Pride will cause them to fall because they cannot accept something for nothing. Unearned grace is anathema to them. The indifferent are too proud to accept charity and too arrogant to extend it. There is nothing more human than an assuring sense of accomplishment. James Lee Beall, in his catechism, *Laying The Foundation: Achieving*

Christian Maturity, teaches on assurance in very broad terms which are very positive. Hear how he describes how much more important justification is compared to assurance:

Assurance is a subjective experience, an inner sure-ness resulting from the exercise of faith. Justification is a judicial decree or declaration of God. Since God cannot lie, and He does not change, this judicial decision makes our restoration to His favor an objective and eternal reality. Justification is the exact opposite of condemnation; it is God's acquittal. The God who has declared the case decided in our favor on the basis of the merits of Christ to whom we are joined by faith and He will never again bring up the matter. For this reason justification gives us peace with God.[vi]

When Beall speaks of assurance in what Christ has done on our behalf it sounds exactly like faith. **Confidence in the** acquittal which the **Living God** has granted us because of Jesus' work and nothing else **is called faith.** Imagine this scenario IF you learned your fate once arriving at the pearly gates: "**Why should you be allowed in**?" you hear over the PA system. The person at the front of the line says, "Because I did my best to be good."   Another person answers, "Because Jesus died for me in my place on the cross and the Father granted me justification simply because I believe it."

Will both enter? IF so, why? If not, why not?

Men fall from grace when they attempt to mix works and grace or earn grace through works. It is either grace or works. You can add nothing to grace. The ordeal of husband and wife Ananias ("grace") and Sapphira (law inscribed on sapphire tablets) in the fifth chapter of Acts makes that clear. When grace and works unified to deceive the Holy Spirit, it destroyed both of them. The urge to add works to grace usually comes from inadequate trust and lack of assurance[vii] in God's decree of justification. If either Ananias or Sapphira trusted the Almighty, they would have come in with honesty and openness.

When deceitful media reports focus on a religious personality's *fall from grace*, they generally refer to evil or "duplicitous" deeds but that is the incorrect use of that term. *Falling from grace* is deliberately making your works the object of your faith. Trying to manipulate the Almighty through your works. When the object of your faith is not the grace or charis of *The*

Cross, you have fallen from grace. Falling from grace is relying on self assurance. The evil and duplicitous deeds are simply called being overtaken in a fault or overcome by sin. A triggered reaction of the old nature. One can recover from falling victim to the old nature as long as their "want to" was truly saved. If the "want to" isn't saved then you might conclude that the individual wasn't either.

CHAPTER SIX

GOD NEEDS TO BORROW YOUR TONGUE

Grace is poured upon Your lips; Therefore God has blessed You forever.
Psalms 45:2b

The grace of Almighty God has been

contracted by the shed blood of Yeshua Jesus to impart the divine nature, according to 2 Peter 1:3-4, into the resurrected spirit cores of every new creation believer.   ***The* Cross, blood, and name** of Messiah Jesus have even established a parental relationship (John 20:21) between the God of Creation and the ungodly who put faith in His Son according to Romans 4:4-5.

The Cross, the blood, and the name have also covenanted the agape love of the Heavenly Father for those who bow at the foot of *The* Cross submitting to the Lordship of Jesus. Let's look at a type and shadow [hint/secret/mystery] of what this inner work looks like in the unseen realm. No Old Testament tongue was more used by the Spirit of Almighty God than Isaiah.

*5 So I said: "Woe is me, for I am undone! Because **I am a man of unclean lips,** And I dwell in the midst of a people of unclean lips; For my eyes have seen the King, The Lord of hosts."*
6 Then one of the seraphim flew to me, having in his hand a live coal which he had taken with the tongs from the altar.
*7 And he touched my mouth with it, and said: **"Behold, this has touched your lips; Your iniquity is taken away, And your sin purged."***
Isaiah 6:5-7

The fire from God's holy altar touched Isaiah's lips and his sins were purged. The fire of God changed the way Isaiah spoke because God's Spirit first changed the way Isaiah thought.

11 I indeed baptize you with water unto repentance, but He who is coming after me is mightier than I, whose sandals I am not worthy to carry. He will baptize you with the Holy Spirit **AND FIRE.**
12 His winnowing fan is in His hand, and He will thoroughly clean out His threshing floor, and gather His wheat into the barn; but He will burn up the chaff with unquenchable fire."

Matthew 3:11-12

When the ungodly put faith in *The* Cross, blood, and name of Jesus (Romans 4:4-5/see chapter two of this book) and submit to His Lordship, the fire of His righteous spirit rushes through our spirits and purges us with unquenchable fire. (Matthew 3:12/Luke 3:17) Just as the fire of the Father's holy altar touched Isaiah's lips and he was instantly forgiven and had his lips sanitized of sin; the ungodly is instantly forgiven, sanctified, [separate by and to God] justified, and purged of sin at the spirit core.

Question: What did Isaiah do to get his lips cleansed and sins purged?

Answer: Nothing!

Isaiah did not contribute to his sins being purged. It was all the work of the Lord of Heaven (Isaiah 6:3) and His fire being applied to Isaiah's thinking, lips, and life. Isaiah witnessed the Lord's holiness and in comparison to God he saw himself as unholy and in bad company. Our natural and devilish practice is to compare ourselves to others and usually those WE THINK are not as _____ we are. Secular humanism, the religion trap, condemnation and false humility conspire against us and we ignorantly collude with them in comparing ourselves to others. On judgment day, the only standard which we will be measured against is Jesus.

Question: What do you think you have to do to have your sins purged?

Can you keep a secret? I hope not. Once you submit to the Lordship of Jesus at the foot of *The* Cross and put faith in His shed blood as payment in full for YOUR sin debt, your sins are instantly judged and punished AT THE CROSS

227

and you are instantly forgiven and your sins are instantly purged from your spirit core by Jesus' unquenchable fire. Do you want to hear another secret? Having your sins judged and punished AT THE CROSS means you don't have to wait for Judgment Day. The Cross is your Judgment Day. Jesus had YOUR SINS, my sins, and the sins of everyone who ever lived and ever will live judged in Him on my cross and your cross. That's right. He was innocent. He is Holy, Holy, Holy. He is perfect. He was an offering for sin but not his own (Isaiah 53:6) because He did not even have slyness in His mouth according to 1 Peter 2:22. His lips were exemplary clean.

He who did not spare His own Son, but delivered Him up for us all, how shall He not with Him also freely give us all things? Romans 8:32

The LORD Yehovah purged our sins through His Son Yeshua Jesus and did so much more for us than we could possibly imagine. This scripture from Romans 8:32 tells us that the same LORD who blessed us through Jesus by purging our sins will also continue to bless us through and because of Jesus with all things which pertain to life AND godliness according to 2 Peter 1:3.

What does all this have to do with the LORD needing to use our tongues? Let's answer that with a portion of what is commonly called The *Lord's Prayer*. The *Disciples' Prayer* is the more appropriate designation for this prayer. It wasn't Yeshua Jesus who needed to pray that prayer. We need disciples need to pray that prayer to this day.

*So He said to them, "When you pray, say: Our Father in heaven, Hallowed be Your name. Your kingdom come. **Your will be done On earth as it is in heaven.*** Luke 11:2

According to 1 Corinthians 3:9, every believer has the opportunity to be a co-worker with the Almighty God. A fellow laborer with the God of Creation? Yes! When Yeshua Jesus taught us the Disciples' Prayer, He made it clear that God's heavenly plans for earth are realized, established, and solidified (redundant I know but makes the point] when WE pray. Now, because we don't know exactly how to pray for what needs to be prayed for or how to specifically pray for particular issues the LORD has a strategy which **can** cause the co-worker prayer to work perfectly. It is call praying in the Spirit, praying in tongues, and **speaking in tongues**.

Let's see a type and shadow of speaking in tongues from the Old Testament through the life and ministry of Isaiah after some time had passed since the fire of the LORD forgave his sins, cleansed his lips, and purged him on the inside.

10 "For as the rain comes down, and the snow from heaven, And do not return there, But water the earth, And make it bring forth and bud, That it may give seed to the sower and bread to the eater,
11 **So shall My word be that goes forth from My mouth***; It shall not return to Me void, But it shall accomplish what I please, And it shall prosper in the thing for which I sent it.*   Isaiah 55:10-11

The Word does go out of the LORD's mouth BUT because He has delegated the dominion and authority over the earth to humanity that Word must pass through the mouths of Spirit filled believers.   His Word works and His angels respond and hearken to that Word even if it comes out of human mouths.

So, God wanted to get His Son into a body so that He could redeem the dead spirit cores of humanity. Isaiah was at first a man of unclean lips and kept bad company. After the fire of Almighty God flowed through Isaiah, God used those words to create the body with which Yeshua Jesus would walk the earth and save the world. The first chapter of Matthew's gospel tells us that it took over four thousand years (forty two generations) from the fall of man for God Himself to have a body. Here is how John's gospel puts it:

In the beginning was the Word, and the Word was with God, and the Word was God.
2 He was in the beginning with God.
And the Word became flesh *and dwelt among us, and we beheld His glory, the glory as of the only begotten of the Father, full of grace and truth.*

John 1:1-2,14

Before the Word of Almighty God became flesh so that His Son Jesus could inhabit a body, Old Testament prophets spoke the small parts of the secret and mystery which God gave them. Eventually, all of those "words" were fused into one incorruptible seed (spore/sperma) and implanted into the womb of a willing virgin servant named Mary. She conceived when the Word seed of Almighty God connected with her human ovum. The result? The birth of a Savior. The birth of redemption. The birth of grace and truth. (John 1:14)

*Therefore the Lord Himself will give you a sign: Behold, **the virgin shall conceive** and bear a Son, and shall call His name Immanuel.*   Isaiah 7:14

Yes, the Word of the Righteous Judge (2 Timothy 4:8) did become flesh and was deposited into the womb of the Virgin Mary allowing for the birth of Messiah Jesus BUT it took the tongues of humans speaking what Almighty God told them to for this to come to pass. So, what if Almighty God used our tongues to pray exactly what needs to be prayed for the remainder of His plans and strategies for the world as well as for your life and family? Imagine the possibilities. When Yeshua Jesus came up out of that grave, He went to His disciples who locked themselves away from the temple guards and Roman soldiers for good reason. The usual practice in quelling rebellions was to destroy the followers after destroying the leader.   What Yeshua Jesus said to these disciples after the resurrection MUST HAVE BEEN important to them as well as to the strategy of Heaven's will and plans being realized and established on the earth.

21 So Jesus said to them again, "Peace to you! As Father has sent Me, I also send you."

*22 And when He had said this, **He breathed on them, and said to them, "Receive the Holy Spirit**.* John 20:21-22

A bit later, He said this to them:

15 And He said to them, "Go into all the world and preach the gospel to every creature.
16 He who believes and is baptized will be saved; but he who does not believe will be condemned.
*17 And these signs will follow those who believe: In My name they will cast out demons; **they will speak with new tongues**;* Mark 16:15-17

After Yeshua Jesus spent forty days visiting with the disciples following the resurrection, He instructed them to wait for the promised Spirit of God to come upon and in them BEFORE going out into the world to preach...

1 the resurrection
2 the repentance of sins
3 the remission of sins

After visiting with the resurrected Messiah for forty days, you would think that the disciples were ready to go preach. You would be wrong. Yeshua Jesus told them to wait until God's Spirit came to reside in them and work beside them in life and ministry. Obviously, the indwelling of the Holy Spirit is critically important to the life of the believer as well as the plans and strategies of Almighty God.

When the Day of Pentecost had fully come, they were all with one accord in one place.
2 And suddenly there came a sound from heaven, as of a rushing mighty wind, and it filled the whole house where they were sitting.
3 Then there appeared to them divided tongues, as of fire, and one sat upon each of them.
*4 And they were all **filled with the Holy Spirit and began to speak with other tongues**, as the Spirit gave them utterance.*   Acts 2:1-4

Following this supernatural event, the prayer meeting poured out into the streets during this pilgrimage period in the Jewish traditions. Hundreds of thousands of Jews and proselytes journeyed to Jerusalem from around the world to be at the Pentecost observance. Some voices came from the crowd saying that these "tongue talking" Galileans were speaking languages which they could not have learned. There were tourists from some sixteen or so nationalities and cultures which heard their own languages coming out of these disciples of

Yeshua Jesus. What did these pilgrims hear?

...we hear them speaking in our own tongues the wonderful works of God."   Acts 2:11

Now that the Spirit of the Almighty has taken up residence in the new creation believer, we can allow Him to use our tongues just as He used the tongues of Mary and the 119 disciples in the upper room. We can yield Him our tongues to pray the wonderful works of Almighty God. We can yield Him our tongues to bring His will and kingdom on earth as it is in Heaven.

If you read Acts 2:6-18 you will get a complete picture of what this event entailed.   It is quite amazing, humbling, and awe inspiring to think that the Almighty God would partner with us to help His kingdom come on earth as it is in Heaven.   A fellow laborer with the Almighty God? That is so cool!   The disciples followed Yeshua Jesus' instructions and waited for the indwelling of the Holy Spirit and the first sermon preached by a Spirit filled man (Acts chapter 2) resulted in over three thousand of the pilgrims coming to faith in *The* Cross, the blood, and the name of Yeshua Jesus.

When it was time for the Holy Spirit to do the same with Gentiles as He had done with the

Jewish followers of Yeshua Jesus, Almighty God sent Peter to the home of a Roman commander in the tenth chapter of Acts to preach *the wonderful works of Almighty God*. When Peter attended the Jerusalem Council in the eleventh chapter of Acts, he recounts the ministry event at the Roman commander's house to the attendees of the council. He repeated to the council what the Roman commander told him which led up to Peter's visit.

13 And he told us how he had seen an angel standing in his house, who said to him, 'Send men to Joppa, and call for Simon whose surname is Peter,
14 who will tell you words by which you and all your household will be saved.'
*15 And as I began to speak, **the Holy Spirit fell upon [these Gentiles], as upon us at the beginning.***
16 Then I remembered the word of the Lord, how He said, 'John indeed baptized with water, but you shall be baptized with the Holy Spirit.'
17 If therefore God gave them the same gift as He gave us when we believed on the Lord Jesus Christ, who was I that I could withstand God?"

Acts 11:13-17

Yes, the Holy Spirit fell upon the Gentiles because some time before Cornelius sent representatives to Joppa to get Peter; Peter was praying [in the Spirit?] in Joppa. Some time before that, Peter prayed [in tongues?] in the city of Joppa and raised a seamstress from the dead. Some time before that while at a city near Joppa, Peter [prayed in tongues?] and healed a man who was victim of [cerebral?] palsy for some eight years. **The plans, and strategies, and will of Heaven** was to fill the Gentiles with the light of Almighty God [Isaiah 42:6, 49:6, Luke 2:32] and He uses praying in tongues to pray the specific pieces of the puzzle to come together to accomplish it.

A man was healed of an eight year palsy in Lydda so that a seamstress' friends in nearby Joppa would know that Almighty God's power was walking among men. The seamstress was raised from the dead in Joppa so that all of Joppa would know exactly where Peter was when the Roman commander's people came looking for Him according to the angel's instructions. What does Almighty God plan on doing in your life once you let Him borrow your tongue?

Understanding what Almighty God has already done for you [justification] and in you [sanctification] will make the transformative understanding of what He wants to do through you [emancipation] simple to accept. Some think that praying in tongues [the prayer language] is for "*special*" Christians or "*extra holy*" believers. If you pay attention to the New Testament especially, you will see that all of Almighty God's children are special and holy. The Cross of Christ makes the ungodly special and extra holy. Our Father has plans for the world and some special things He wants to do in and through your life and mine and loves to borrow our tongues to pray the perfect will and strategies of His plans.

What do you say? You in?

It took me over a year to receive the overflowing presence of the Holy Spirit with speaking in tongues because the people around me did not know how to teach receiving the prayer language. They spoke in tongues in droves but did not have the hang of teaching it. It is really simple. First, you take care of first things first and pray the prayer of repentance to receive faith for salvation and then ask and receive the gift of the Holy Spirit.

8 But what does it say? "The word is near you, in your mouth and in your heart" (that is, the word of faith which we preach):

*9 that **if you confess with your mouth the Lord Jesus and believe in your heart that God has raised Him from the dead, you will be saved**.* [rescued from God's judgment on sin]

10 For with the heart one believes unto righteousness, and with the mouth confession is made unto salvation.

11 For the Scripture says, "Whoever believes on Him will not be put to shame." Romans 10:8-11

*"If you then, being evil, know how to give good gifts to your children, how much more will your heavenly Father give the Holy Spirit **to those who ask** Him!"* Luke 11:13

And they were all filled with the Holy Spirit and began to speak with other tongues, as the Spirit gave them utterance. Acts 2:4

A prayer this simple will have your sins judged at the cross:

"Lord, I confess that Jesus is the Son of God and that you raised Him from the dead. Your Word says that if I say and believe this with my heart, I will be rescued from your judgment on sin. I thank You Heavenly Father for saving me and making

me one of your children. Thank You Father."

A prayer this simple will help you receive your prayer language and loan Almighty God your tongue:

"Now that I am a reborn child of the Almighty God, I ask you Heavenly Father to give me your Holy Spirit as You said in Luke 11:13 that You give to any of Your children who ask. I yield my tongue to You to give me the utterance of the Holy Spirit prayer language with the evidence of speaking in tongues. Thank You Father."

You will "hear" or "feel" words in the center of your "heart." They will sound like your thought voice. Simply breathe normally inhaling through the nose and exhaling through the mouth as you praise your Heavenly Father for the gift of the promised Spirit. Start speaking the words which you hear or feel and let the Holy Spirit flow using your tongue. You see, you are still in control of your tongue. The Holy Spirit is a gentleman. He won't violate your free will. He won't force himself. He flows through a yielded vessel. With His help you can pray so that the Almighty's kingdom comes on earth as it is in Heaven.

When the fire of God purged your spirit at salvation, He perfected your spirit (Hebrews 10:14, 12:23) where the real you lives and has put you in position to receive all that your Heavenly Father has prepared for you.

I find it absolutely mind boggling that the Almighty God of creation needs my tongue. I am blown away to think that He would enlist my assistance in His plans and strategies for this world in any way. In religion, the man-made barter system, it is easy to think of prayer as something we have to do. Some kind of work. In this tongue yielding labor of love with the Almighty God, prayer is something we get to do. Me and God? You and God? Talk about a dynamic duo. What an honor!

Read your Bible frequently and regularly but don't bog down with the volume of your reading. Three verses read fifteen to thirty times will take root better, sooner, and stronger than fifteen chapters read once. Slow down and get more out of it. You will know when to read fifteen but don't burden yourself with condemnation even if you go a day without reading a verse at all.

Beware the religion trap! You didn't do anything to get right with Almighty God so don't let condemnation and false humility deceive you into thinking your performance is what qualifies

you to run boldly to the throne of grace. The
work of salvation is none of ours but all God's.
As Charles H. Spurgeon said, "It's all of grace."
The Hoppers sing, *Grace Will Always Be Greater
Than Sin*. It also will always be greater than
religion. Religion is not what you think it is. It is
man's way of approaching Almighty God. Yeshua
Jesus is God's way to approach Him. Religion
and false humility teach us that **when** *we sin we
have an advocate with the Father* and we think
that is Bible truth. Actually, the Word of
Almighty God says in 1st John that **IF** *we sin we
have an advocate with the Father*. Religion and
false humility deceive us into thinking that we
are sinners saved by grace BUT the Word of
Almighty God calls us sinners only BEFORE we
put faith in *The* Cross, blood, and name of Yeshua
Jesus.

AFTER *The* **Cross**, the Word of Almighty
God calls the former ungodly who put faith in
Yeshua Jesus saints. **Not sinners but saints!**
Religion, false humility, and condemnation teach
us that we will and even must sin incessantly but
the relationship we now have with Almighty God
encourages us with the encouragement, "...*IF we
sin*..." When we realize that at the moment of
salvation the Almighty God MADE US
RIGHTEOUSNESS (2nd Corinthians 5:21) without

us expending one finger of effort, then we are as righteous now as we ever will be. Ephesians 2:7 says that the grace of salvation isn't the beginning of grace. Our Father gave us all of it.

and to put on the new self, created to be like God in true righteousness and holiness.

Ephesians 4:24 NIV

Beware the religion trap! Take another look at the **Spirit Core Paradigm Shift Following Faith In The Cross** graphic on page vi. You will also find a version on page 246 with scripture references. Sin will keep your identity founded in the column on the left. Guess what? Religion, false humility, and condemnation will do the same devilish thing. The older brother in the *Parable of the Prodigal* represents religion and false humility. He was working for something which he already had. He didn't need to work for it because His father had already given it to them both according to Luke 15:12.

Religion can deceive you into attempting to work for what you cannot earn –Almighty God's amazing grace. Once you agree with the Word of God about the grace which He has BESTOWED on you already, false humility will deceive you into thinking that faith in Jesus isn't really that good. Your focus on what you used to be will have you accepting God's goodness with bashfulness. The unholy trinity is rounded out with condemnation which will attempt to deceive you into thinking that you are not what the grace of Almighty God's Word says that you are so....

Beware the religion trap! Church people and God's people need to be delivered from religion just as the ungodly need to be delivered from sin.

20 But you, beloved, building yourselves up on your most holy faith, praying in the Holy Spirit,
21 keep yourselves in the love of God, looking for the mercy of our Lord Jesus Christ unto eternal life.   Jude 20-21

Praying in tongues, praying in the Spirit, and speaking in tongues [however you decide to label it] builds up your faith according to this scripture. You don't have to work for faith or do some sort of Biblical gymnastics to build your faith. Yes, memorizing the scriptures has an amazing affect on your mindset and faith but keep in mind that even the faith which we need to give Almighty God (Romans 4:16) so that He can treat us with grace [like we never sinned or ever had the sin nature] comes from Him (Romans 12:3, Galatians 2:20, Ephesians 2:8) and Jude 20-21 tells us that by praying in the Spirit we can increase that faith. Why is praying in the Spirit an act of faith? Because it reminds us that He can use our tongues not because we are good enough BUT BECAUSE HE IS MORE THAN GOD ENOUGH.

The Spirit Core Paradigm Shift
Following Faith in *The* Cross

From

To

Deformed (corrupted)
1 Corinthians 15:50
2 Corinthians 11:3
Galatians 6:8

Transformed (perfect)
John 17:23
Hebrews 12:23
1 John 4:18

Eternal Death
Ezekiel 18:4
Matthew 25:41
2 Thessalonians 1:8-9
Philippians 3:17-19
Revelation 20:14; 21:8

Eternal Life
John 3:16, 36
Romans 6:22
Ephesians 2:8-9
2 Peter 1:11
Revelation 20:6

Enemy of God
Proverb 8:36
Luke 20:34
Romans 8:7
James 4:4
Ephesians 2:12
Colossians 1:21

Child of the Living God
Matthew 5:9
Luke 20:36
John 12:36
Romans 8:16, 21
Galatians 3:26
Ephesians 2:15-16

Far From God
Ephesians 2:2-3
Ephesians 2:11-19
Ephesians 5:6
Colossians 3:6

Made Near To Him
Ephesians 2:11-19
Hebrews 7:19
Ephesians 5:8
James 4:8

Condemned
Ezekiel 18:4
John 3:18
Jude 4

Justified
John 3:16-18
Luke 18:13-14
Romans 5:1, 5:9, 8:1, 30

Wicked	Righteous
(thinking)	(mind of Christ)
Acts 2:23	Romans 5:18-19
Romans 1:27-32	1 Corinthians 2:16
Colossians 1:21	2 Thessalonians 1:3-5
2 Thessalonians 3:2	1 John 3:9, 5:1,4,18
1 Corinthians 5:12-13	1 Peter 3:12, 4:18
1 John 3:12	Revelation 12:10-11

Wickedness	Righteousness
(position in satan)	(position in Christ)
Matthew 13:38, 22:15-18	Ephesians 1:3, 2:5-6
Luke 11:39	Romans 8:16-17
Romans 1:27-32	Colossians 3:1-3
2 Thessalonians 2:8	2 Peter 1:1-4
1 John 2:13-14, 5:19	1 John 5:18-20

Guilty	Innocent
Matthew 23:18	Luke 23:14 imputed
Romans 2:5, 3:19, 9:22	Romans 3:26
1 Corinthians 11:27	Philippians 2:15
Ephesians 2:3	1 Peter 3:18
James 2:10	

At War With God	Have Peace In God
Romans 8:7	Romans 1:7, 5:1, 8:6
James 4:4	Romans 14:17
Ephesians 2:15-16	Ephesians 1:2

Dead In Sin	Alive In The Spirit
Ephesians 2:1	Luke 15:24
Ephesians 2:5	Romans 6:11-13
Colossians 2:13	1 Corinthians 15:22

Sinner
Proverb 11:31
Ephesians 2:5
Colossians 2:13

Saint
Romans 8:27
1 Corinthians 1:2
2 Corinthians 13:13

Sinner "Saved? By Grace"
Not in the scriptures. Once
a sinner is saved by grace,
the Word ONLY refers to
this person as a saint. The
identity has changed. Now
the behavior catches up by
first the belief catching up.
Just do SAY it!

Joint Heir* With Christ
Romans 8:17
Galatians 3:29
Titus 3:7
Hebrews 1:14
James 2:5
1 Peter 3:7

*Does "joint-heir" put us a couple levels below Christ?

Imprisoned in darkness
Psalm 107:10-11
Isaiah 60:2
2 Corinthians 4:4
2 Peter 2:4

Free In God's Kingdom
Romans 8:2
Ephesians 5:8
Colossians 1:13
1 John 2:8

Victim of Darkness
Colossians 1:13

Victorious In Jesus
Romans 8:2, 37
1 Corinthians 15:57

Dead In Sin   [D.I.S.]
Romans 6:13
Ephesians 2:5
Colossians 2:13

Dead To Sin? [D2S?]
Romans 6:2, 11, 13
Romans 6:14-18
Colossians 2:9-15
Hebrews 10:10
1 Peter 2:24
Revelation 1:5, 12:10-11

ENDNOTES

---

[i] Genesis 15:5-6

5 Then the Lord took Abram outside and said to him, "Look up into the sky and count the stars if you can. That's how many descendants you will have!"

6 And Abram believed the Lord, and the Lord counted him as righteous because of his faith.

Holy Bible, New Living Translation ®, copyright © 1996, 2004 by Tyndale Charitable Trust. Used by permission of Tyndale House Publishers. All rights reserved.

2 Chronicles 20:7

7 O our God, did you not drive out those who lived in this land when your people Israel arrived? And did you not give this land forever to the descendants of your friend Abraham?

Holy Bible, New Living Translation ®, copyright © 1996, 2004 by Tyndale Charitable Trust. Used by permission of Tyndale House Publishers. All rights reserved.

James 2:23

23 And the scripture was fulfilled which says, Abraham believed God, and it was imputed unto him for righteousness: and he was called the Friend of God.

[ii] Biblesoft's New Exhaustive Strong's Numbers and Concordance with Expanded Greek-Hebrew Dictionary. Copyright © 1994, 2003, 2006

  Biblesoft, Inc. and International Bible Translators, Inc.)

[iii] From the Library of Congress Website

The American astronomer Edwin Hubble made the observations in 1925 and was the first to prove that the universe is expanding. He proved that there is a direct relationship between the speeds of distant galaxies and their distances from Earth. This is now known as Hubble's Law. The Hubble Space Telescope was named after him, and the single number that describes the rate of the cosmic expansion, relating the apparent recession velocities of external galaxies to their distance, is called the Hubble Constant.

www.loc.gov/rr/scitech/mysteries/universe.html

[iv] Biblical grace is anything but a license to sin. For example, Jude warned of the heretics of his day who were "turning the grace of God into licentiousness" (Jude 1:4). Those heretics, like their counterparts today, portray God's grace in such a way that leads people to think they can continue sinning with impunity.

(From DavidServant.com; The Limits of God's Grace)

[v] Based on the translation of Louis H. Feldman, The Loeb Classical Library.

[vi] Lee Beall, James. Laying the Foundation (Kindle Locations 1117-1121). ReadHowYouWant. Kindle Edition.

[vii] Lee Beall, James. Laying the Foundation (Kindle Locations 1193-1195). ReadHowYouWant. Kindle Edition.

NOTES

GERALD McCRAY

Made in the USA
Columbia, SC
08 March 2018